Shoot the Indian:
Media, Misperception and Native Truth

Edited by Kara Briggs, Ronald D. Smith and José Barreiro

Illustrations courtesy of Frank Salcido

An annual reader of the
American Indian Policy & Media Initiative
Buffalo, New York

American Indian Policy and Media Initiative
1300 Elmwood Avenue
Buffalo NY 14222-1095
www.AmericanIndianInitiative.buffalostate.edu

Interior layout: Maisie MacKinnon
Cover design: Kristin Johnson
Printed in the United States of America
ISBN-13: 978-0-9795981-0-4

Shoot the Indian: Media, Misperception and Native Truth, is the annual reader of the American Indian Policy and Media Initiative.

Publisher's Cataloging-in-Publication
(Provided by Quality Books, Inc.)

Shoot the Indian : media, misperception and Native truth /
  edited by Kara Briggs, Ronald D. Smith and José
  Barreiro.
  p. cm.
  Includes bibliographical references and index.
  ISBN-13: 978-0-9795981-0-4
  ISBN-10: 0-9795981-0-9

  1. Indian mass media--United States. 2. Indians of
  North America--United States--Public opinion. 3. Mass
  media--United States. 4. Public opinion--United States.
  I. Briggs, Kara. II. Smith, Ronald D., 1948-
  III. Barreiro, José.

  P94.5.I532U6 2007   302.23089'97
                            QBI07-600144

Dedication

Dedicated to John C. Mohawk whose mentorship inspired the founders of the American Indian Policy and Media Initiative, whose corn soup fed us and whose early support for the Initiative gave it wings.

Artist Acknowledgment

Frank Salcido is Dené from the Standing House Clan. He is a painter, who uses positive themes to showcase contemporary and traditional Indian lives with color and imagination.

He graduated from the both the Institute of American Indian Arts and the College of Santa Fe in 1978. His art has shown in galleries in Santa Fe; Aspen, Colorado; Cody, Wyoming; San Diego, California, New York City and Portland, Oregon.

Salcido has worked as a graphic artist in printing companies. His work has also given him adventure such as when he worked as a National Park Service ranger in New Mexico and Wyoming; as part of a railroad tie gang for the Santa Fe Railroad; as a teachers' aide on the Navajo Reservation; as a dancer touring Texas with a Northern Plains powwow troupe from the National School Assemblies. Now he works as a certified medical assistant in an oncology office in Beaverton, OR, outside Portland where he and his wife live.

His employment supports his art, which for six years he has primarily sold at the world-famous Santa Fe Indian Market and through Bonnie Kahn's Wild West Gallery in Portland, Oregon. His focus is on ledger art, for which he picked up a taste while working in Grand Teton National Park in Wyoming. He likes to put old style American Indians in contemporary settings.

In Salcido's hands, converging stereotypes are props which he uses to show Indian humanity and humor large on the canvas. Some Salcido pieces depict the simple joy of family life, such as Indian children watching a western in the drawing titled *Shoot the Indian,* from which this book takes its name.

Many of his paintings and drawings muse on possible meetings of historic figures, named and unnamed, because in Salcido's world view indigenous peoples from around the globe are more closely related than one-dimensional histories tell. A Navajo plays flute for a Pharaoh; a Northwest Coast leader and an Aztec leader stand side by side. On a ceramic horse he painted for the Trail of Painted Ponies series in 2006, a Navajo medicine man and a Tibetan monk are collaborating on a sand painting of the entire world.

"I am trying to connect the pyramids of the Aztecs and the Egyptians," Salcido said. "People back then used to travel around a lot. In New Mexico at the Pecos National Park where I used to work, there are dentalium and other shells from the Northwest Coast. They say they used to come down and trade with us. We have a lot of parrot feathers from down south too."

The American Indian Policy and Media Initiative thanks Frank Salcido for his contributions to this book.

Table of Contents

Notes on Style

In editing this book choices were made concerning punctuation, syntax and other style elements to reflect a growing body of Native considerations.

In particular, the term Indian Country was edited out of many chapters. The catch phrase popularized in newspapers such as *Indian Country Today* and *News From Indian Country* is too non-specific to be used when referring to specific lands, such as a reservation land or ceded territory. Ideologically, Indian Country can mean all of the Americas, which are aboriginally Native. But increasingly, this phrase is wrongly being used in media reports about specific tribal nation's lands. In these cases, as in most cases in this book, the specific names of particular pieces of real estate were preferred to the broader term.

Also eliminated was the phrase "Indian casinos" and replaced generally by "tribal casinos." This is an important semantic and legal distinction. The legal right to operate a casino is held by tribal nations, not by individual tribal members.

In identifying the tribal affiliations of individuals, we chose to set off their tribe with comas following their name. We write the person's name and then offset by comas his or her tribe. We do not consider tribal citizenship to be parenthetical, as we read in some publications which insert paragraph marks around the tribal nations' name. We consider tribal citizenship to be a central fact to an individual's identity, and to express that we use the style that newspapers use to identify a source's hometown. This is the style largely used by Native media and also by the small handful of newspapers that have developed guidelines for syntax and punctuation concerning Native American coverage.

We capitalize the word Native, when written to mean Native American. Native is a term that has grown increasingly popular in tribal communities and in the Native media over the last decade. Native is capitalized, as used in these publications. Other media inexplicably struggle with this capitalization. Many like the *Wall Street Journal* write native, lowercase, and American, uppercase. We think that confuses the public understanding of Native peoples. We also think that may be the editorial wish of some publications.

We use American Indian, Native American and Native, and sometimes Indian, relatively interchangeably. All are inaccurate. The only accurate terms are the specific tribal names. Speaking internationally, as many chapters do, we fall back on these terms.

– Kara Briggs, Editor

Preface:
A Crucial Time for Indian Country to be Heard

– By Retired U.S. Senator Ben Nighthorse Campbell –

I go to a lot of Indian meetings where tribal leaders and advisors discuss their most important issues, value each other's cultures and present their viewpoints. There is a lot of good Indian thinking going on—even in the midst of very difficult problems and many challenges and attacks upon tribal rights by well-organized and hostile groups.

One of the most stimulating gatherings I have attended was held at Buffalo State College, in that famous western New York city that is the eastern gateway between Indian Country, the United States, and our Canadian First Nations relatives.

The founding meeting of the American Indian Policy and Media Initiative in June 2005 focused on how to build and communicate an effective defense of historical truths, and the legal and self-governance rights of tribal peoples in the United States.

It was hosted by a couple of veterans of Native journalists, Tim Johnson and José Barreiro, and put together a refreshing core of very sharp minds. These included tribal leaders such as Chairman Anthony Pico of the Viejas Band of Kumeyaay Indians, who gave a powerful presentation, and critical thinkers among well-established Native journalists such as columnist Suzan Shown Harjo, reporter Kara Briggs and others.

The ensuing discussion—full of clear thinking and creative energy—gave me reason for hope that our dignified and resilient Native peoples in North America will succeed in their quest to survive and prosper.

Tribal nations in North America face serious dangers to their communities and national interests. From where I sit, it clearly seems that the media arena is a major area of contention where our cultures, peoples and representative institutions must make a vigorous and principled stance.

There are good signs, not only at Buffalo, but also at other media organizations, such as the Native American Journalists Association, which is working to increase the number of Native American journalists.

Various academic programs, including major ones at Harvard University and at University of Arizona, among others, are also conducting research into economics, politics and law of tribal nations. But the promise of the American Indian Policy and Media Initiative is its focus on a nationally active, real-time engagement to better inform and educate the American public.

These are the same folks who elevated our national American Indian newspaper, *Indian Country Today*, these past five years. (A book of their opinion and perspective essays, entitled, *America is Indian Country*, came out Fall 2006 from Fulcrum Publishers, gives a great indication of their depth and range.) The Initiative coalesces some of the very best and brightest researchers and writers to help the American public come to a more informed and accurate understanding of American Indian peoples and our issues.

The decency, resiliency and wise cultural cornerstones of our American Indian governments are not visible to most Americans. Stereotypes abound. Even more dangerous, a palpable shift in attitudes from positive to negative, what Barreiro called "a shift in public metaphors," is clearly media-driven.

Often media outlets are being unwitting conduits for professional media manipulators representing anti-Indian groups.

Johnson emphasized the need for tribes to get involved in supporting productive think-tanks, such as this one in Buffalo, and to get busy with national media strategies that can turn the negative tide.

The main point of the session was that the public perception created by media almost always sets the pattern for public policy. Buffalo State College Professor Ronald D. Smith presented results from a recent Initiative research studies that tracked the media influence on public attitudes.

The studies show a remarkable residue of public sympathy for Indian People, which can decline as tribes ignore the importance of participation in the media discourse or can improve as the public gains increased exposure to accurate information about Indian peoples and their histories.

There was a great scene about halfway through the epic 1982 film *Gandhi*. In one of his many campaigns, Gandhi—I paraphrase from memory—found himself surrounded by powerful enemies and flanked by the British army when several young college students break through the battle lines to his camp.

The great leader asks them, "And what are you young people studying?" "We are becoming journalists," they reply. Gandhi clasps his hands together. "Thank God," he exclaims. "Now we have won our struggle."

The key to American Indian survival lies in our ability to educate, and to win hearts and minds on behalf of our fundamental quest for freedom and justice. All American Indian leaders and people of good will should support our ethical journalists and brilliant communicators.

Ben Nighthorse Campbell, Northern Cheyenne, is a former member of the U.S. Senate. He currently serves as Senior Policy Advisor to Holland and Knight.

Public Perceptions v. Tribal Realities

– Remarks by Anthony R. Pico –

*Former Chairman of the Viejas Band of Kumeyaay Indians,
speaking to the founding roundtable meeting of the American Indian
Policy and Media Initiative at Buffalo State College on June 15, 2005*

The task you have undertaken is of vital importance to all Indian Country. The future preservation and prosperity of American Indians will not be decided in the halls of Congress or state legislatures, or in the U.S. Supreme Court. It will be decided in the court of public opinion. That's why I'm encouraged with American Indian Policy and Media Initiative.

How we are viewed in the eyes of the nation—and our ability to deliver our message to the public, the press, elected officials and federal and state policy makers—is of crucial importance to our grandchildren, their grandchildren and generations of our people yet to be born.

Perception is reality. Truth is our ally. If we don't take the steps necessary to promote an accurate image of American Indians, if we do not tell our story completely and accurately to everyone and anyone who will listen, then the pillars of economic, social, governmental and political success that tribes have begun building over the past thirty years will come crashing down around us.

Sadly, I fear cracks are already growing in the foundation.

It's been three decades since American Indian tribes began what continues to be a very difficult climb from the depths of poverty and neglect at the hands of a failed system of federal paternalism. We have yet to reach the sacred mountain a place where we envision economic, legal and social equality with our non-Indian neighbors.

A progressive and liberating federal policy of Indian self-determination that began in 1970 with the administration of President Richard Nixon—coupled with U.S. Supreme Court rulings and congressional action recognizing the right of tribes to engage in government gaming—has brought tremendous and largely positive change throughout Indian Country.

For the first time in generations some Native nations have the economic and political strength necessary to hold our destiny in our own hands. We can finally begin to heal the wounds inflicted by generations of genocide, of enslavement, of forced removal from our Native lands, and all the many injustices that make up our tortured history since European settlement of this country.

For the first time in modern history tribal governments can begin taking their rightful place among the federal, state and local governments of this nation and resume control over our own affairs.

From the Indian perspective, it's a time to rejoice. So where are the good news stories?

Instead of applauding tribal sovereignty as crucial in lifting Native nations out of generations of poverty, the public, the press, Congress, state legislatures and the highest court in the land are seeking to tax our governments and erode our right to self-reliance and self-determination as if Native sovereignty were some kind of plague sweeping the nation.

Instead of crediting tribal governments for creating 533,000 jobs and economic development—both on reservations and in surrounding non-Indian communities—the public, the press, Congress and state legislatures portray economic progress on Indian lands as somehow encroaching on communities, clogging roads and desecrating the environment.

With some 230 tribal governments operating more than four hundred casinos, our spirit of generosity, charitable giving and cooperation with local communities is being miss-characterized by media coverage of a handful of disputes. Given our history I'm absolutely amazed at how much effort tribes have made to accommodate demands by state and local governments.

Why are Native governments derogatorily referred to by the media as "cash-rich Indian tribes?"

Who is perpetuating this myth of the rich Indian? Despite the economic gains in Indian Country, many tribes still live in Third World conditions.

- For example: 25% of our people live below the poverty line.
- The majority of our people lack adequate education and health care.
- Our reservations are plagued by suicide, drug and alcohol abuse, diabetes, and many of other dietary and health problems.
- Another 40% of our homes lack adequate plumbing and kitchen facilities.

The people who will suffer most from the rich Indian stereotype will be the poor Indians. The few successful gaming tribes will become an excuse for the federal government to further retreat from its treaty obligation to tribal nations, including the more than three hundred that don't have gaming.

Does the country welcome participation by American Indians in the political process? No. Newspapers seem to imply that we have too much influence, that we are bullying and abusing the system. We face accusations that we "flaunt our casino riches."

Native cultures—our traditions, our governments and our political systems—were here long before Europeans arrived in this country. Yet Native American tribes are still not regarded as sovereign nations with a responsibility to provide for our peoples' education, law enforcement, fire protection, clean water, roads and sewer systems and all the other services non-Indian communities take for granted.

We are not now—nor have we ever been—properly recognized as people indigenous to this country with culturally rich heritages that dates back to ancient times.

Until recently, we were largely an invisible people—victims of a kind of benign neglect. Throughout much of the twentieth century, we disappeared, not only from the news but also from school textbooks.

Generations of non-Indians grew up believing we were either extinct or on the way to becoming so. Out of sight, out of mind. The last Indian mentioned in a California textbook died in 1880. We were frozen in the images of the cowboys and Indians of the frontier, obstacles to America's Manifest Destiny.

We have for so long been isolated by our poverty and the remoteness of our reservations. So the stereotypes came into play. Iron Eyes Cody shedding a tear at the shore of a polluted lake.

And today? Today gaming is the context within which Indians are defined. It's as if we all suddenly crawled out from beneath a craps table, our loin cloths replaced by green aprons.

We are in the eyes of non-Indians looked upon as businesses, corporations, perpetrators of gambling, casino operators.

It's unfortunate that the engine driving the unprecedented growth on Indian lands is being fueled by casino gambling. It's unfortunate that no other method of economic development would work on largely remote tribal reservations, lacking infrastructure and often far from major population centers.

The American public has a lovers' quarrel with wagering. According to an American Gaming Association survey released earlier this year:

- 80% of Americans believe gambling is acceptable
  for themselves or others.
- One-fourth of Americans visited a casino in 2004.
- 89% of the American public said casinos
  near their communities met or exceeded their expectations.
- Two-thirds of the American public said casinos helped
  more than hurt, their communities.

Meanwhile, gambling has become the nation's latest flu epidemic. The national hysteria is over the perception, thus far unfounded, that most reservations are suburbs for casino sites. This despite the fact that there have been fewer than forty requests for off-reservation gambling operations under provisions in the *Indian Gaming Regulatory Act* since the federal legislation was enacted in 1988. Most of these were uncontroversial, contiguous land annexations approved by local jurisdictions.

The truth of the matter is, most attempts to establish off-reservation casinos have been made not by tribes, but casino speculators and state governors and legislators in the hope of generating economic development or tapping into tribal government revenues to help alleviate budget deficits.

As I said in the beginning, in the game of politics and public opinion, perception is reality.

I find it odd that while it is perfectly legitimate for commercial casinos, race tracks, racinos, video lotteries, card clubs and off-track betting parlors to operate in cities, the public and politicians turn up their collective nose at the notion of tribal governments locating a gambling operation in their midst.

So be it. Gambling will forever be a politically risky endeavor for tribes. Unlike other "moral" issues such as abortion and gay rights—debates that divide this country along conservative and liberal lines—gambling is opposed by both sides of the congressional aisle and from both ends of the political spectrum.

Gambling, from a public relations perspective, is a no-win proposition.

Tim Johnson asked that I briefly discuss ballot referendums in California which eventually led to passage in March 2000 of Proposition 1A, the constitutional amendment which allowed Class III compacted gaming on tribal lands.

It was a heartfelt victory for Native Americans in California and throughout the country. Both Proposition 5 and 1A generated "yes" votes from 63% of the voters. It was an overwhelming victory for tribal self-reliance.

The referendums upheld pre-election polling by the California Nations Indian Gaming Association. The association's statewide surveys were revealing. Among the highlights were the following statistics:

- Regional support for tribal self-sufficiency through gaming ranged from 68% in the Sacramento area to 8% in San Diego County.
- When asked why they would vote for Proposition 1A, 75% of those surveyed cited reasons of fairness and equity. Said one respondent "Indians have had a raw deal for years. It's their land; let them do what they want on their land."
- Also among the positive benefits of Indian gaming, 85% of the respondents identified jobs for both Indians and non-Indians, and 79% said that tribal government gaming provided a controlled and policed gaming environment.
- The survey showed that 73% found Indian casinos an attractive form of entertainment, and 79% agreed that tribal gaming kept betting dollars in California.
- About 64% believed that tribal government gaming was adequately regulated by the tribes.
- 62% said tribal gaming operations took into account local environmental requirements and were in compliance with local government regulations.

We were confronted by a campaign financed by organized labor and Nevada's commercial gambling. Opposition from Nevada's gambling industry was beneficial to the tribes as the public displayed strong disfavor toward Las Vegas casino companies being involved in California politics.

A majority of California voters, from 54 to 57 percent rejected the idea of expanding casino gambling beyond Indian reservations.

In retrospect, it's clear that California voter support was not so much an endorsement of gambling as it was approval of tribal self-reliance and self-sufficiency. Californians were not embracing gambling and casinos. They were embracing the tribes.

The surveys confirmed that Californians continued to see Indian-operated gaming as an issue of justice, fairness and a means of creating economic independence for tribal governments.

It was, however, a qualified support. The public wanted a portion of revenue sharing funds to be used in an education and treatment program for problem and pathological gambling.

And what remains very significant is that the public opposed gaming beyond tribal lands.

Since passage of the *Indian Gaming Regulatory Act of 1988*, no issue has generated as much public and political sentiment against American Indians as the uproar over efforts by a handful of tribal governments to acquire off-reservation land for gaming purposes.

The growing political and public fear that tribal gaming will spread unchecked throughout the nation and penetrate urban areas.

Wade Blackdeer, vice chairman of the Ho-Chunk Nation of Wisconsin, said of a House bill to limit off-reservation gaming, "This legislation appears designed to address a problem that does not exist."

Headlines and political grandstanding notwithstanding, tribes are not for all intents and purposes able to engage in off-reservation gaming.

Nevertheless, the concern being generated by the potential proliferation of tribal gaming has seriously eroded the political capital of American Indian nations. It has generated divisiveness among American Indian tribes. It has prompted leaders of both the House Resources Committee and the Senate Committee on Indian Affairs, to consider amendments to *Indian Gaming Regulatory Act*, and the federal process dealing with acquisition of trust lands.

This is neither the time nor the place to debate the merits of these issues. That is left to other forums and symposiums.

What is important to those of us gathered today is that we recognize that the press coverage and Congressional scrutiny being given to tribes and tribal gaming is symptomatic of a public backlash generated by a false and tarnished image of Native Americans.

We must also recognize that if we do not become proactive in our dealings with the public and the media, the consequences will be unrelenting attacks on tribes and tribal sovereignty.

So what do we do? I have a few thoughts. It's against Indian custom to talk about ourselves. There is a powerful disincentive for parleying with the media. However, we've got to step up to the plate.

One of the most difficult things I've had to overcome is fear of talking to the media. It's a pretty common fear, especially among Indians. For Indians, speaking to the press is akin to being a traitor. The press is still viewed through a prism of the past. Newspapers are seen as purveyors of propaganda used to exploit tribes. They're at least partly responsible for perpetuating negative stereotypes, by interpreting American Indians through ethnocentric mirrors of European superiority.

We need to get beyond that.

We must direct more of our resources to public and media relations. National and state tribal gaming associations and individual tribal governments must elevate public and media relations to a budgetary status equal to government and legal affairs.

We need to recognize the distinction between public relations and press relations.

We must, as tribes, unite in the funding and development of a long-term education, information and advertising strategy. Our goal would be creating an accurate, deep and contemporary image of American Indians in the minds of the American public. This may include branded documentaries, institutional advertising and specialty publications. A positive, nationwide image of Native Americans will go a long way in blunting the impact of negative stories in *Time* magazine and the *Wall Street Journal*.

We must, as tribes, create a national clearinghouse of research and information, including statistical data, on pending and continuing issues of importance to tribal nations, whether it be sovereignty, taxation, land-in-trust issues, off-reservation gaming, or natural resource development and preservation.

We must not simply react to the press and media reports, but create the message. Individual tribes, as well as state and national trade associations, must tell our story, through means such as producing guest opinion columns on local, state and national issues. We must learn to communicate with the public, the press and the elected officials.

Newspapers are the first line of communications with the public. Yet too many individual tribes are hiring highly paid public relations firms with no communication skills and no experience in newspaper journalism. Forcing newspaper reporters to deal with public relations firms in gathering information is tantamount to declaring war with the press. Tribes need to hire people with newspaper experience who can write and understand the complexities of a newsroom.

Tribes must reach out to the business pages of local, state and national newspapers and magazines. The story of tribal gaming is largely one of job creation and economic development. Yet too often coverage is by the statehouse or political reporter. Stories on tribal economic development rarely, if ever, fall on the business pages where it often belongs, and where more positive stories are generated. It is difficult to criticize job creation and economic development.

We must encourage and fund efforts to develop Native American curriculums in the schools.

And, we must do what we can to encourage more Native American men and women to enter the field of journalism. One day, I hope to open my daily newspaper and see a nationally syndicated column with an American Indian byline.

I have taken much of your time. But this is a topic near and dear to my heart. It is also one of great importance.

We face many challenges. I hope, together, we can make a difference.

▼ ▼ ▼

Anthony R. Pico, Viejas, served more than two decades as chairman of the Viejas Band of Kumeyaay Indians. Under his leadership, the Viejas Band developed the multi-million dollar grossing Viejas Casino as well as the Viejas Outlet Center and two RV parks. A national model for diversification of a tribal economy, the band also is the majority shareholder of the Borrego Springs Band and a partner with three other tribes in a Residence Inn by Marriott on Capital Hill in Washington, D.C.

Forty Years After Kerner

– By Kara Briggs –

The media report and write from the standpoint of a white man's world. The ills of the ghetto, the difficulties of life there, the Negro's burning sense of grievance, are seldom conveyed. Slights and indignities are part of the Negro's daily life, and many of them come from what he now calls "the white press"—a press that repeatedly, if unconsciously, reflects the biases, the paternalism, the indifference of white America. This may be understandable, but it is not excusable in an institution that has the mission to inform and educate the whole of our society.

—Kerner Report, 1968

Like the Miner's Canary, the American Indian marks the shift from fresh air to poison gas in our political atmosphere. Our treatment of the Indian, even more than our treatment of other minorities, marks the rise and fall in our democratic faith.

—Felix Cohen, 1953

I n the months before the start of the current millennium, I—then a newspaper reporter—was meeting with an editor, when out of nowhere she asked, "What have Indians ever contributed, anyway?"

In 1999 I was one of a couple hundred Native American journalists who worked in mainstream daily newspapers, and in my newsroom I had been tapped to write an article about Indians in the year 2000.

The editor had previously told me she wanted this story and others in the series to be provocative.

I proposed a story that I deemed important in expressing the state of Indians who at the turn of the millennium were reclaiming cultural practices and knowledge that had been all-but wiped out in the last four hundred years by the genocidal pressures of America. The story was about a Paiute weaver who through her dreams was remembering ancient styles of weaving, which her tribe had not practiced since before she was born. Only the oldest elders of her tribe could remember and identify the uses of her weavings.

To me this was provocative, considering, as one historian told me, that Congressmen from 120 years ago, who had legislated for our extinction, would be "surprised as hell" to know that Indians and their cultures were still alive in the twenty-first century.

This didn't meet the editor's standards of provocation, though her question provoked me into remembering how at the birth of the U.S. the Haudenosaunee Confederacy informed our Constitution, our formula for confederated states and our ideal of universal suffrage.

I told her: "Democracy. We contributed American democracy."

The Commission on Civil Disorders

I remembered this incident, one of many similar in my nearly twenty years in mainstream daily newspapers, as I reread the Kerner Report in preparation for editing this volume.

And I was amazed anew at the insight that members of the National Advisory Commission on Civil Disorders had nearly forty years ago into race and the news media.

The commission had been convened in 1967 by President Lyndon Johnson to find a smoking gun responsible for riots in black communities of major American cities. The ensuing report turned its attentions to the vast racial divide between black and white in social institutions such as the news media.

Fry Bread Feast © 2003 Frank Salcido

It blamed the media, along with other civic institutions, for stirring up fear against black communities. The media did this by, among other things, quoting white officials and business owners while ignoring black residents, calling for legislative steps to quell the violence without trying to understand the black residents' perspectives, and staging riotous acts for the camera.

That the report failed to acknowledge the brown majority of the Americas, or that few women existed beyond the white-gloved society pages, was an oversight of the era. Yet its themes continue to play out in media coverage today of indigenous-related issues from the largely Indian immigration from Mexico and Central America to the growing influence of tribal nations in politics and society, in part because of success in casino gaming.

This occurs despite the notion of objectivity, which was the rallying cry of news reporters through the middle of the last century. Objectivity was the presumption that journalists–who are still majority male and white—could divorce their personal biases and opinions from their work. Maybe that was possible when covering the community meant the white newspaper men covering the white community.

But objectivity fails when the reporter is out of his depth—reporting in a community with a radically different history and culture. How can American journalists who may only be able to name ancestors back to their grandparents understand Native people, like one elder from the Confederated Tribes of Warm Springs in Oregon who said that his tribes' ancestors go back eight hundred generations.

In my view, and that of many journalists I've worked alongside, our personal experiences and knowledge so influence the way we see the world—and therefore the way we see stories—that the best we can hope to attain in our journalism is fairness.

Institutional Racism

The advent of casino gaming has been a particular sore point to white reporters and their editors, whose abhorrence belies an unusually large streak of Puritanism.

When Native Americans complain about reporting, talk often turns to the 2002 articles in *Time* magazine by Don Bartlett and James Steele titled "Who's Cashing In at Indian Casinos."

The articles decried the dangers of casinos—without

acknowledgement of the majority of tribes which are too far from urban centers to make casinos viable or the majority of gaming tribes that have used their casino income to better their communities. Tribal America was uniquely unified in its response to this reporting, which nonetheless took home a variety of white media awards.

Native leaders who objected to the *Time* articles may not realize that Bartlett and Steele were regular teachers at regional and national journalism conferences, influencing a generation of would-be investigative reporters. The problem with Bartlett and Steele's methodology is they decide on a supposition, then go out and report to prove it, other Pulitzer Prize winning investigative journalists have told me.

The process is exactly the opposite of the common-sense approach of reporting on a potential story before reaching a conclusion about what it means. This is the method most beat reporters use on stories.

In the same year Susan Masten, then chairwoman of the Yurok Tribe in northern California, pled with reporters from metropolitan newspapers to travel to her reservation to witness an ecological disaster unparalleled in the history of the region.

A reported 77,000 adult Chinook and endangered coho salmon were dead or dying in the dried up Klamath River. It was an ecological disaster of Biblical proportion, and certainly one that lacked precedent in equally long Yurok oral tradition. Yet it would take years for any but Northern California media to report the fish kill.

In 2001, a year earlier, the national media had been all over another story on the Klamath River. You may remember the footage of the silver-haired southern Oregon farmers breaking into a federal dam. The farmers were protesting a federal order to stop releasing river water for irrigation in order to save species of salmon listed as threatened under the Endangered Species Act. They would in time break into the dam and turn a spigot to illegally divert water.

By 2002, newly inaugurated Vice President Dick Cheney intervened on behalf of the predominantly Republican farmers in this swing state to make sure the government science favored the irrigators. With water flowing again through irrigation ditches in time for the 2002 growing season, spawning salmon returned to a dry river bed. It would take until 2007 for the *Washington Post* to look into this government conspiracy.

But in 2002, Susan Masten dialed the phone of every journalist she knew asking them to cover the situation. They refused because they didn't have time, because their editors wouldn't give them the time, because CNN had beamed a different story into their newsrooms. Seeking publicity, Masten decided to hold a peaceful protest at the same dam near Klamath Falls, Oregon. While Yurok elders marched, federal workers locked their office doors.

In doing that, Masten said, they were leaving the Yuroks without access to the public restroom which had been afforded the white farmers even though their earlier protests turned violent. Still there was only local coverage for this national story.

"I never knew what institutional racism was until then," Masten said.

The Gaming Obsession

Since the 2005 Jack Abramoff bribery scandal, newspapers, weeklies as well as dailies, have refocused their attentions on tribal gaming—with what I can only describe as glee.

One editor at a large daily newspaper smiled like a school boy as he told me of plans to reopen the long abandon Indian beat, so, he said, they could investigate tribal casinos. At a journalism conference dinner, I caught an editorial page editor from a small Connecticut daily snickering as he told the black ombudsman of a large Midwest newspaper about the rise in his state of some of the wealthiest tribal gaming enterprises in the U.S.

His editorials show his contempt for tribes based on their casinos.

The language and tone in a growing number of daily newspaper stories, such as ones that appeared in the *Oklahoman,* the *Detroit Free Press* and several newspapers in New York State, took dramatic turns in 2006 toward the rhetoric of anti-Indian activists.

Tony Thornton's article "Tribes Profit from Status," which appeared in the *Oklahoman* in July, punctuates an explanation of the 1887 *Dawes Act* with the stand-alone exclamation, "That gives the tribe immense advantages." In describing a new gaming venture, Thornton uses phrases such as "once again" to denote a tired resignation about new economic development by Oklahoma tribes. The tone is radically different from that used by most newspapers when reporting on non-tribal development.

Thornton's article failed to discuss the numbers of jobs likely to be created by these enterprises, as reports about other economic development usually do.

The *Detroit Free Press* dedicated a three-day series by reporter

Jennifer Dixon to describing how Michigan did a poor job negotiating its compacts with the state's gaming tribes, and "lost" three hundred million dollars in possible revenues. The series also repeatedly blamed tribes for spending the revenues, which a careful reader of the series would understand belonged to the tribes and not the state of Michigan.

Part of the problem with Dixon's writing and her editors lack of oversight are the short-hand explanations that, "The state can't collect taxes from tribes because they are sovereign nations."

Without clearly explaining, or clearly understanding themselves, the roots of that sovereignty and the treaties that the U.S. made with tribes at its founding and as it expanded across the continent, it's no wonder that sources such as Republican Michigan State Rep. Fulton Sheen can proclaim their ignorance of federal Indian law in the *Free Press* by saying "Why are they treated any differently? To me, it's a travesty."

Days after publication, newspapers, radio stations and TV news were repeating abbreviated versions of the series—stating that tribes were taking money out of state coffers—leaving out the details that an insightful Free Press reader could ferret out from beneath the rhetoric.

The failure in these and many other examples of reporting on Indians has its roots, some say, in long-standing misunderstanding of tribal nations by mainstream America.

The Individual v. The Tribe

Alan Parker, the Chippewa Cree director of the Northwest Indian Applied Research Institute at Evergreen State College, has said that the great divide of between tribal nations and mainstream America results from a disparity in iconic stories.

For mainstream America, the archetypal story is the heroic individual, pulling himself up by his boot straps. The story of tribal nations is always about us, the group, the people, the tribe.

In America, us—as in communism, as in Enron, as in city hall—is always suspect. And in the twenty-first century, red-baiting is aimed at tribal America.

The Kerner Commission was most remarkable in its media observations for linking the absence of journalists of color from newsrooms to the media's fear mongering toward the black community.

Since the Kerner Commission, the focus of journalists has been to change the media from within by increasing the number of journalists of color.

Organizations such as Unity: Journalists of Color, the Native American Journalists Association (NAJA) and the Maynard Institute for Journalism Education were founded to improve journalism by encouraging diversity in the media through training, job fairs and holding the feet of corporate media to the fire over failures in their hiring practices.

No doubt great gains were made by journalists of color such as Joe Boyce, a black policeman recruited to join the *Chicago Tribune* in the 1960s, who retired as an editor at the *Wall Street Journal* in 1999, and George Benge, a Cherokee reporter who covered the American Indian Movement occupation of Alcatraz in 1969 and who retired as a Gannett executive in 2007.

Robert Maynard became publisher of the *Oakland Tribune* in the 1980s. He also founded the Institute that bears his name. And he was among the journalists of color who convinced the American Society of Newspaper Editors (ASNE) in the late 1970s to make a commitment to increasing the number of journalists of color in newsrooms.

In 1978 ASNE set a goal of bringing the percentage of minorities employed in newspaper newsrooms up to parity with the population by the year 2000. At the time, the percentage of journalists of color was 3.95%.

Muted Voices: Frustration and Fear in the Newsroom, was a report released by the National Association of Black Journalists in 1993. It found that newsroom managers were not committed to retaining and promoting black journalists and that about one-third of black journalists believed that discussing race in the newsroom would damage their chances for advancement.

By the mid-1990s the growth in hiring of not only black journalists but also Native, Asian American and Hispanic journalists had stalled around 13% of newspaper newsroom staffs.

Credibility

In 1998, two years before the year 2000, when racial diversity in newspaper newsrooms was supposed to have reached parity with the national population of people of color, ASNE called a series of meetings to discuss the obvious failure to reach this goal.

I represented the Native American Journalists Association at the first of several meetings that ASNE called. This one was at the old Freedom Forum office in San Francisco on a beautiful winter day. The room was filled with prominent journalists of color. But the collegial excitement of seeing old friends quickly turned to anger when it became clear that ASNE wanted to back off its goal.

The editor representing ASNE started the meeting by asking us what we could do to pick up the responsibility for diversifying the news media. He suggested pipeline programs, scholarships, mentorships, all ideas straight out of the playbook that journalists of color organizations had used for years.

The journalists scoffed, shook their heads in frustration and expressed so much disdain for this blame shifting that the editor from ASNE sat down. It may have been the plan to change moderators, as was later suggested. But clearly the editor had lost the respect of the audience. Felix Gutierrez, who as a vice president of the Freedom Forum was host, took the podium and began facilitation of a historic conversation.

For two decades journalists of color had looked to industry leader ASNE to guide its own membership past racism and toward inclusion of journalists and news from diverse communities. ASNE's adoption of this goal, however slippery, had given us an argument to make with our own editors about the importance of media diversity.

But with an approaching deadline that certainly would not be met, it appeared that the association of the nation's highest ranking news editors wanted to wash its hand of the socially challenging objective. Some might argue that ASNE was only brainstorming. If so, it was a funny way to do it.

ASNE had always had problems with this goal. Many editors didn't think ASNE should have taken on the goal of diversifying newsrooms. Many newspapers didn't participate in the voluntary census. Privately, I, among other journalists of color, questioned the credibility of reporting.

Journalists of color in some newsrooms kept count of the numbers reported and the numbers that could be identified on staff. One senior Asian American journalist told me that his large metro daily would have had to count summer interns and administrative assistants to reach the diverse news staff it claimed. A self described white woman with distant Indian ancestors objected to her big city newspaper listing her as one of its minority staff. She believes her objection was ignored.

During the 1990s the clarion call from journalists opposed to diversifying newsrooms was: We aren't going to hire people of color who aren't qualified. But Bob Maynard, through the Institute of Journalism Education, which now bears his name, had given our answer a decade earlier in his goal of eliminating the phrase "not qualified enough" from the lexicon.

A Long Ways Off

In 2001 the National Association of Black Journalists released *Voices of Anger, Cries of Concern: Some NABJ Views of the Retention Problem—and Some Solution,* which opened with a letter addressed to ASNE editors from then-NABJ president Will Sutton. He wrote in the second paragraph: "The newspaper industry took in about six hundred journalists of color in 2000 and watched 698 leave."

ASNE continues to release its annual census, which despite its faults is the best count of journalists of color that exists. As it has for the past decade, the percentage of journalists working in newspaper newsrooms lingers around 13%.

I'm not sure that this number can climb, given the changes in the industry. In recent years we have seen at least one publicly-held newspaper chain lay off journalists of color at a higher rate than white journalists. We have also watched the decline in newspapers as commercial advertising has decreased. This has caused a drop in newsroom staffing, generally.

Most egregiously in recent years non-journalist shareholders held up newspaper chains such as the late Knight-Ridder and the Tribune Co. for ever-larger profit margins.

To hear these shareholders speak, you'd think they were going to be bereft on the street if newspapers didn't cut a larger profit margin. Where do the cuts come? They come in news that matters—reporting on international issues, on diverse American communities and on other important news. Cuts have also come in layoffs of news staff. Journalists of color have been significantly represented, probably overrepresented, in these numbers.

There are other reasons why we may not reach our goal of parity. The rise in sophisticated online news outlets has drawn many talented journalists out of newsrooms. The growing reliance of communities of color on ethnic, Spanish-language and tribal media as their primary source of news. The notion of parity is ever-changing as America grows more racially diverse faster than we expect. A 2006 U.S. Census report found that nearly half of the nation's children under five years are racial or ethnic minorities.

Nonetheless, we cannot back off the goals for diversifying mainstream news outlets if we want our news media to remain credible to an increasingly diverse America.

Kara Briggs is associate director of the American Indian Policy and Media Initiative at Buffalo State College. She is a long-time daily newspaper reporter and a columnist for Indian Country Today.

American Indians in the American Mind

— By José Barreiro —

For those of us monitoring the media fight between a compelling and realistic American Indian profile and those who would mar or otherwise diminish that profile, the past two years have been a time of critical decisions. More than ever, tribal leaders and their spokespeople are in the crosshairs of criticism from journalists, pundits and politicians who espouse ideas that are fermenting in the public arena.

Tribal leaders and opinion leaders in Indian country often complain about the depiction of their peoples and issues in the media. Often, this refers to the lack of depiction, which in good part results from a lack of Indians in the media. Also missing from the news are American Indian experts who could accurately speak about the ways that Indian-related news affects America in general from the *Cobell v. Kempthorne*, the class action suit over government misuse of the land and money of more than half a million individual tribal members to the scandal over Inmate No. 27593-112, aka lobbyist Jack Abramoff.

Beyond invisibility, tribal leaders also point to the outright hostility of some of the media, often skillfully driven by groups that are opposed to Indian interests. This happened long ago when the United States was settled by European immigrants. It is happening again today at great risk to contemporary tribal nations. Organized anti-Indian groups have become a voice and force to counteract. Largely, these interest groups wrap themselves in the American flag and intone the mantra of "one nation under God" to presume that the American Indian nations of this land should not, or cannot, any longer exist. These groups, which often outnumber tribal peoples in their localities, are serious in their efforts to pressure politicians through the media. Cases in New York and Connecticut, Wisconsin, and Montana give evidence of their organizing.

As tribal governments and communities have expanded their base of rights and economic expectations during the past two decades, they have made many gains. But this empowerment has also unleashed a wave of fear and loathing in various societal groups. It has stirred significant ideological currents and applied political power. In some cases, as in New York State, we have seen well-organized groups attack tribal rights so consistently and virulently that the journalists lifted their message whole and carried it as their own.

One anti-Indian campaign framed the issue so effectively that the news media, and even the U.S. Supreme Court, believed the lie that the entire population of Central New York was traumatized by tribal gains.

This hoodwinking by special interest groups combines with the media's own sin of lumping all Indians together, for good and for evil, a practice that often affects Indian news coverage. Since the notorious Jack Abramoff lobbying scandal, which involved a mere handful of Indian tribes, anti-Indian efforts have intensified substantially. What is certain post-Abramoff is that the collective image of Indian peoples took a serious blow in the media coverage of 2005 and 2006. Many opinion makers, who are relatively ignorant of Indian issues, professed positions with destructive intent toward tribal nations. Most of this went unchallenged outside Indian Country. Native news outlets, such as *Indian Country Today* and some Indian columnists in the mainstream media did respond, but they generally have a much lower resource base and far less outreach capability than major media outlets.

Talk among media pundits is shifting back to the termination era of the 1950s, when the Bureau of Indian Affairs and Congress conveniently declared that tribes in Oregon, Wisconsin and other states no longer existed. Eventually, tribal nations such as the Klamath in Oregon and the Menominee in Wisconsin won back recognition after hardfought legal battles. But talk of termination has never died out, particularly in times when media and elected leaders have organized against tribal nations.

Now, pro-termination arguments are being carried by the anti-Indian groups and aligned with at least one wing of punditry on the right. They have even garnered support of pandering politicians on the left. They provide provocative arguments in nationally important newspaper columns. Involvement by any Indian entity in a scandal or questionable situations generally results in a negative shift in the national image of Indians.

Posted on the Web site of the anti-Indian organization One Nation is an article titled, "Schwarzenegger, tribes on collision," by Alan Murray of CNBC. The article's main thrust is to cheer on the Terminator as he shakes down the tribes for all they are worth.

Farther north on the Pacific Coast, the United Property Owners of Redmond, Wash., recently announced that they would merge with One Nation, which is based in Oklahoma, to form a larger, nonpartisan anti-Indian group called One Nation United. Publicity from the new organization indicates that it will have approximately 300,000 members, and be represented in all fifty states.

This uniting of anti-Indian groups is a good reminder of how these groups consistently stir the pot against tribal nations nationally. One Nation United is one of a fast-growing coalition of organizations intent on the destruction of tribal freedom throughout the United States. These groups seek to gain both a national profile and influence for their cause. Their movement is poised to become increasingly dangerous for tribal nations.

Indian Country leadership ignores it at peril to Indian peoples.

The anti-Indian movement's arguments against tribal rights, and particularly against the sovereign jurisdictions asserted by American Indian nations, is finely honed. The modern anti-Indian movement has been incubating for more than thirty years. Growing from gripe sessions among non-Indian residents on reservations, the groups united with convenience store operators and other business owners who feared competition from growing tribal enterprises. These smooth operators are in cahoots with toothy-grinned state governors, legislators and mayors. Together, they are getting ready for the good old American dance of usurping tribal land, eroding tribal rights, and imposing taxes on tribal enterprises.

Waging a War of Perception v. Reality

In America circa 2006 public metaphor is everything. The national metaphor for American Indians is turning dramatically as tribal nations come to the fore. Political anti-Indian groups and the news media are fear mongering in old ways that are severely damaging Indians in the American psyche.

One Nation and other groups of the same ilk and politicians from various states are now onto something: The power of the Indian image in the American mind can be damaged or even reversed from what positive perceptions exist. The "noble caretaker of the plains" per elementary school textbook fame, or the reality of Native nations seeking justice in America, gives way to the image of greedy, special-interest casino kingpins. Say it enough times, and it becomes the overriding public metaphor.

Or as Jeff Johnson, the Republican candidate for attorney general of Minnesota in November 2006, demonstrated you don't even have to say it. In the days before the election, Johnson's TV ad portrayed a long-haired, head-band-wearing Indian man as a perpetrator of identity theft for a split second before shifting to the good people of the state, i.e. the blond suburbanites who Johnson presumably would have represented exclusively had he won the election.

The antagonist idea is to denigrate the image of law-abiding Indians and legitimate tribal governments in the public mind. Replace these honest images with a new picture—the American Indian getting a free ride, the American Indian conniving and thieving.

The point here is not that these perceptions are, at least incidentally, grounded in truth, for some among the half-dozen tribes that were seriously duped by Abramoff and his minions. But, in the media, the perception of these isolated incidents easily becomes the common silhouette of 562 federally recognized American Indian and Alaska Native peoples, who have specific histories and accomplishments.

Although always distinct culturally, this group is not so small anymore if we go by the 4.4 million U.S. Census figure. The complex amalgam of Indian Country can be dangerously reduced in the American mind by the shameful actions of a few nations, such as disenrollment of large numbers of members over politics. The media has a way of overemphasizing attention on these cases without giving their full context, a practice that erodes the credibility of all Native nations. These troubling instances are aggravated in the media by journalists' "herd mentality" and their need to present quick (read: superficial) reports on complex issues.

Gaming Regulatory Act: Focus of Unrest

Some pundits have come quickly to the arena, armed for combat with "the Indians." As the Abramoff stew heated up in 2004 and 2005, the attacks turned on the general intent of the *Indian Gaming Regulatory Act*. This act is consistently misinterpreted by media giants such as the *Wall Street Journal* and the *National Review*. Although the tribes that Abramoff fooled have not been indicted for illegal acts, the journalistic knives are flying over the supposed rampant corruption among all gaming tribes.

When it comes to American Indians, all manner of cheap shots are tolerated, and these don't just come from the political right. From the left, liberal publications strive to prove their credibility by beating up on tribal sovereignty and self-government without taking time to understand that these policies have, for the first time in U.S. history, allowed some measure of justice for tribal nations.

On February 19, 2006, the normally balanced *New York Times* ran a front page spread that unfairly characterized an entire Mohawk community in northern New York State as aiding and abetting drug smuggling by family members and friends. In her article, "Drug Traffickers Find Haven in Shadows of Indian Country," Sarah Kershaw of the *Times* described the kind of drug smuggling operations that are practiced along the length of the borders with both Canada and Mexico, as well as along huge holes in coastal security. Yet Kershaw breathlessly hyped the smuggling on the Mohawk reservation at Akwesasne to be the result of tribal sovereignty and Indian peoples' weak morality, while ignoring how severely despised this criminal element is by the large majority of reservation families, the Mohawk tribal government, and the traditional longhouse.

Such casual stereotyping as that demonstrated by the *New York Times* could ultimately prove more destructive to tribal sovereignty than the Abramoff scandal.

The language of termination is increasingly heard from media writers. Prominent writers such as Holman Jenkins Jr., a member of the editorial board of the *Wall Street Journal*, rile against "defunct tribes" and their "enduring nonsense of Indian 'sovereignty'." Jenkins bemoaned the surprising resilience of any "Indian sovereignty," pining for an illusive termination from Indian friend, Senator John McCain, (R-AZ). "[B]ut even that may come," Jenkins hopes, because the "backlash" against tribal sovereignty is "already on the way."

By late 2006, tribal leaders were reeling from a *Cobell* settlement plan in McCain's Senate Bill 1439 that would forgive all past and future claims of government mismanagement of tribal lands. This forgiveness, if it were to slip through Congress (which tribes were organizing against at this writing), would give rise to a happy forgetfulness, and once again raise the question of why tribes—which the *Sacramento Bee* termed in mid-2006 "businesses" not "nations"—have unique rights.

There is a serious argument in America today. It's being heard across the country as a chorus that will continue to croak a dangerous mantra. The media herd is too willing to repeat it as truth. While Indian enemies envision the complete deconstruction of Indian sovereign nations, the fight in Congress—and by extension in the hearts and minds of the American public—becomes paramount.

Remember John Kerry's "flip-flop" image? True or not, it stuck. Again, it was just a tactic. The damage was done through a public relations strategy built on repeated innuendo. The same happens to Indian issues.

It is not fair and follows no logic, but it manipulates, intending to diminish any gains made by Native tribes. Thus, the push is on to portray the tribes as lobbying nightmares, enclaves of valueless societies that roll in their ill-gained casino dollars. This is cultural preparation that's being set up in preparation for the political kill. It's the swift-boat attack of the Indian issue polemic. Indians are "rip-offs, "cheats, supporters of corrupt lobbyists, "special interests," and impediments to America. The only things in the way is that pesky American Indian sovereignty and reservations (read: real estate) over which these "phony" governments exercise control.

Controlling the American Indian Message

Established circles of American Indian opinion makers, national organizations and tribal nations need to be empowered to organize far-reaching campaigns to generate in the public, and even among American media professionals, a more comprehensive understanding of Indian Country.

Proper and realistic representation in media is crucial for the protection of American Indian peoples' rights, both those that are inherent and those affirmed by treaties, litigation and legislation. The way situations and issues are covered, by which I mean how the media comes to interpret Indian realities, increasingly drives public policy. Issues that can help or wreak havoc on American Indian tribal life are decided too often by the clamor of negative public attention, not by reason and precedence.

For a positive Indian campaign to work, it must encompass a coalition of Native and non-Native individuals and organizations. It should lead to dialogue within Native circles about the fundamentals of the media and the means of successful, consistent delivery of Indian ideas and facts to the media. Tribe by tribe, regionally and nationally, we need to grow in understanding of media and media strategy. We need to learn the skills of the craft.

There is much to be said in this discussion. In light of substantial economic growth—which triggered huge prosperity for some tribes, moderate income for most others, and sizable headaches for almost all—distinctions among American Indian situations must be understood. The explosive financial nature of the gaming path is not an option for nearly 70% of tribes, while destitution and poverty remain prevalent. Nevertheless, the controversy, hostilities, and stereotypes generated against gaming tribes affects all of Indian Country.

A Time for Redirection

So here are some ideas about how we, as American people of conscience, can redirect the dynamics I've discussed.

Tribal leaders must study the ideologies and language of groups whose mission is to end tribal sovereignty if they are going to provide an effective counterbalance. The messages from tribal leaders—affective elder voices are key in this effort—must be distributed through all means that our telecommunication age provides. Understanding the changing nature of media, particularly with the continued growth of the Internet, is critical to new era communications.

American Indian nations must beware of attempts to pit wealthy gaming tribes against poor, land-based tribes. We must resist the Indians-fighting-Indians game that government and media will push us into if they can. One solution would be for tribal coalitions to buy national television time to introduce America to American Indians—and for tribes to support in whatever ways they can. The overall humanity of Native peoples must be conveyed to the broader public, a public that is largely predisposed to favor the mythic Indian, even as the importance of tribal economic growth must be explained to the public.

Most of all, such campaigns must let America see and hear the real Indian America. Such communications would celebrate the Native family, while exposing the public to the most superlative tribal ways of building family and community. The role of American Indians in the U.S. military and among the ranks of veterans must be communicated to the broader America. Such a campaign would be most successful if launched in tandem with American Indian philanthropy, even as a growing number of wealthier tribes help less fortunate tribes to seek greater self-sufficiency.

To report accurately on Indian issues respect for the history of tribal nations on their lands is critically important. A failure to understand the unique role of tribes on their own lands and their practice of culture on these lands dooms us to misunderstanding, and diminishes the legitimacy of tribal claims. It even, over time, feeds the desire of some to dehumanize tribal peoples, as we see in sports team mascots and advertising for corporations such as Anheuser-Busch. These stereotypes are natural backdrops to the noisy polemics of public policy about tribal nations. It is time for factual information to come to inform public opinion. The contest for hearts and minds is the crucial test that will tell if tribal political and economic successes will be sustainable.

This is the most critical task facing the collective Indian Country. For it to succeed, it must be pursued proactively, week by week, community by community.

The campaign to dislocate the Indian image in the public mind and relegate it to the outer edges of American consciousness—along with other "troublemakers" or anti-American elements—puts in peril Indians of all generations. Indians must do their very public opponents one better, by using the strengths of truth, fairness and law, all of which are on our side.

José Barreiro, *Taino Nation, is an author, scholar and intellectual activist with thirty years dedicated to the service of Native people. He serves currently as Assistant Director for Research at the Smithsonian National Museum of the American Indian.*

Explaining Sovereignty Through the Media

— By Mark Trahant —

Indians face the issue of low visibility in the media, but the Internet has changed things in many remarkable ways. At the Unity: Journalists of Color convention in 2004, I asked President Bush about tribal sovereignty. (If you haven't seen the clip, just Google my name.) Let's just say President Bush had a hard time articulating sovereignty.

But what's extraordinary about the question and the answer that followed is how the interaction became a permanent piece of furniture on the Internet. It remains a presence three years after the event.

The "sovereignty clip" has been a top-viewed hit on VH-1. It's been featured on the *Colbert Report* and can be found on many Web sites such as www.youtube.com.

On the Internet, perhaps more than any other medium, Native people have a way to respond to stories in real time. Then, when something is out of kilter, or just wrong, that message can get out instantly. And permanently.

Of course the world has changed beyond the Internet. More Native Americans are in newsrooms sitting at keyboards, thinking about what makes news—and then writing the story. We are, more than ever, defining what is considered news.

Sometimes these definitions are cast in tribal publications, such as the *Navajo Times*, the *Sho-Ban News*, the *Yakama Nation Review*, the *Apache Scout*, or the *Seminole Tribune*. There are some three hundred reservation-based publications, and another three hundred written and edited for Native Americans living in cities. Add to that another one hundred magazines, thirty radio stations, and several television stations, both broadcast and cable-only systems, and a growing number of Internet 'zines.

In the Native press—and I use the term broadly—there is a lot of space on page one. Most Native media efforts serve two communities: a tribal community wanting to know what's going on as well as the larger community, region, state or neighborhood.

Sometimes, tribal media serves as a tip sheet, clueing the clueless big city newspaper into a real story. Tribal (and intertribal) news media has come of age in many communities where the next edition is as eagerly awaited as a camp crier.

Native American journalists also define "news" at the regional and national levels with publications such as *Indian Country Today* and *News From Indian Country*, the syndicated radio newscast *National Native News* and, even better, through the ordinary, thoughtful discourse of the live radio call-in show *Native America Calling.*

Back in the so-called mainstream press, it's important to look beyond the stories and peek at the bylines. There you'll see names like Kara Briggs, Jodi Rave, Matt Kelley, Seth Prince, Charlie LeDuff and so many other excellent reporters and writers from Indian Country. Or consider Mike Kellogg, a Navajo and publisher of the *Stillwater Daily News*, and president of the Native American Journalists Association.

Bylines Matter

A few examples: Kara Briggs, who was then a local government reporter at the *Oregonian* in Portland, is a Yakama Indian and a former president of the Native American Journalists Association. When tribal leader Joe DeLaCruz died, for example, she convinced her editors to let her do a story. She traveled to the Quinault leader's funeral and then wrote an essay that explained why DeLaCruz was important; she put a Native leader into broader context. She explained to readers why DeLaCruz mattered to all people in the region, not just tribal members.

Jodi Rave writes about Indian issues for Lee Enterprises, a midwestern newspaper chain. I'll say right here and now: she ought to be considered for the Pulitzer Prize for national or explanatory reporting for her series on American Indian trust funds.

Those who have read Rave's series should better understand one of the most complicated, underreported stories in our generation. Here is her lead from one story in the series:

> Picture this piece of land four, three, even two centuries ago.
>
> Eighty acres of hardwood forest in Wisconsin's upper reaches. Ojibwe country. Maybe they hunted there. Maybe they fished. But they didn't own the land; most tribes didn't think anyone could own the land.
>
> Today, that land—on the Lac Courtre Oreilles Reservation— likely hasn't changed. It's still 80 acres of hardwood forest, still Ojibwe country.
>
> But you could fill a small city with the number of tribal citizens sharing ownership in the 80 acres: At one point, the local Bureau of Indian Affairs office struggled to simply keep track of the parcel's 2,400 owners. And they can all be traced to Git-chi-i-kwe Sr., and the U.S. government's controversial introduction of land ownership to tribal citizens.

Rave gets to the heart of a serious problem. Why can't the federal government account for the land it's supposed to hold for Indian people? The answers lie in the complexity of how Indian land is owned and how it's passed down to heirs. Jodi Rave makes that connection. She tells a story that gives a reader important context. Rave and many Native writers, reporters, editors and producers, build on a rich tradition of storytelling.

Indian Country is full of such stories, stories that ought to be told with respect. There are complicated histories that defy traditional grab-and-go journalism, stories with roots deep in history. They are stories about nations whose governments predated those of the United States, stories about cultures, languages and people.

Why should journalists care about such things? Well, let's talk a little about journalism philosophy.

Responsible Journalism

More than fifty years ago, a group of scholars said journalists ought to be careful when telling stories about groups other than their own.

A dozen intellectuals, led by University of Chicago Chancellor Robert Maynard Hutchins, crafted a remarkable criticism of the nation's press. The panel linked press performance to that of our democracy because, they said, the news media reaches all corners of our society, shaping our views about what's important.

"Responsible performance [of the news media]...means that the images repeated and emphasized be in total representative of the social group as it is," the scholars wrote in their 1947 report, *A Free and Responsible Press*. If the media does it right, they said, citizens will be, "exposed to the inner truth of the life of a particular group, and they will gradually build up respect for and understanding of it."

A Free and Responsible Press was published at a time of uncertainty. Newspapers and radio were faced with a new competitor, television. No one was certain how that would change the values of news. A half-century later, we are again at a time of change. The Internet is forcing us to think about our values and about how the news media impacts democracy.

That brings me back to the Internet, and the prospects for what's ahead. The Hutchins report was published during a time of media upheaval. There was this new thing called TV, and it was causing a lot of uncertainty. Sounds a lot like today.

That is why it is so important that Native Americans define this new medium.

We need a new sovereignty movement—a sovereignty of storytelling.

Mark Trahant has been writing about Indian Country for three decades, starting as editor of his tribal paper, the Sho-Ban News *in Fort Hall, Idaho. He is now editorial page editor of the* Seattle Post-Intelligencer. *He is also chairman of the Maynard Institute for Journalism Education's board of directors. Trahant is a member of the Shoshone-Bannock Tribes.*

The First Pundit:
John Locke's Wild Indians Mythology

– By James Adams –

"The wild Indian, who knows no Inclosure."

–John Locke

acist stereotypes have distorted federal Indian policy and Supreme
Court decisions on Indian law from the nineteenth to the twenty-
first centuries. The description of Indians as "lawless, uncivilized
savages" dates to the earliest days of first Contact. Scholars say the
imagery reached full flower in the justification for Spanish conquest
of America given by Juan Ginés de Sepulveda, "the father of modern
racism," in the famous disputation at Valladolid in 1550.[1]

The stereotype reappears in a long line of U. S. Supreme Court
opinions, many revived as precedents well into the twenty-first century
in decisions of the Rehnquist court.

University of Arizona law professor Robert A. Williams blames the
mind-set of the European settler, which he calls "racial dictatorship."[2]
The condemnation is well deserved, but the roots of the Indian
stereotype go even deeper than this historic American bigotry toward
people of color. The image of the Indian as a primitive hunter-gatherer
was the essential element, theoretically and legally, for the Anglo-
European appropriation of the continent.

This story starts with John Locke (1632-1704), one of the most
influential of modern political philosophers. With little dispute he could
be called the theoretician for the English settlement of America. Indian
intellectuals instinctively regard him as their nemesis.[3] Locke's *Second*

Treatise of Government lays the foundation for modern representative government and free-market economics.[4] But to a remarkable degree, Locke shaped his classic text to justify the colonial dispossession of Indian land.

Locke had more interest, theoretically and personally, in the American Indian than any other political philosopher in the European Great Tradition. He read and cited the Jesuit Relations and Spanish writers on Native tribes to support his theory of the emergence of civil society. But he also used the intelligence for his professional duties. Decades before his treatise took shape, Locke was a major functionary in the British colonization of North America.

Coexistence to Dispossession

Early in Locke's career, he became close adviser and member of the household of the politically powerful Anthony Ashley Cooper, who after the overthrow of the Stuart line became first Earl of Shaftesbury. As a young physician, Locke saved the life of Lord Ashley (as he was then known) through a dramatic liver operation. The two worked closely on Ashley's colonial investments in North America. In 1663, Ashley became lead member of the "Lords Proprietors" of the Carolina colony. He and Locke produced an elaborate constitution for the new colony, blending semi-feudal land distribution with an extraordinary degree of religious toleration, extending even to Natives.[5]

In 1672, Ashley became president of the Council of Trade and Foreign Plantations. Locke was sworn in as its secretary in 1673, charged with watching the affairs of all the English colonies in North America, from Hudson's Bay to the Caribbean. His biographer says he considered a visit to Carolina.[6] He even invested his own money in a settlement in the Bahamas, a major step for the economical philosopher. The Council was dissolved two years later, just before the outbreak of King Philip's War, the most serious of the indigenous challenges to the eastern seaboard settlements.

Locke showed a strong interest from the start in the Native peoples of the "New World" but one can see an evolution in his policy from coexistence to dispossession. In guaranteeing religious toleration, the *Fundamental Constitutions for the Government of Carolina* contains the fascinating statement, "The natives of that place, who will be concerned in our plantations, are utterly strangers to Christianity, whose idolatry, ignorance or mistake gives us no right to expel or use them ill." Still, these Natives were included in a provision giving any seven persons "agreeing in any religion" the right to constitute a church.[7]

But by the time of the publication of the *Two Treatises of Government* in 1689,[8] Locke had worked out a theory that justified the transfer of American land from its first possessors to the English settlers. This theory was entirely separate from the doctrine of Christian Discovery.

For Want of Improving

The State of Nature, Locke argued, resembled the condition of the American Indians; "thus in the beginning all the World was America." Natural resources were a commons, and each man could appropriate as much as he needed by mixing his labor with it, without hurting other men "since there was still enough, and as good left" (33:3). In fact, it was the addition of labor that created value, making land worth ten, a hundred, even a thousand times more than it did "without any Husbandry upon it." For proof, Locke offered the condition of the Indians who, in his version, were ignorant of agriculture:

> There cannot be a clearer demonstration of anything, than several Nations of the Americans are of this, who are rich in Land, and poor in all the Comforts of Life, whom Nature having furnished as liberally as any other people, with the materials of Plenty, i.e. a fruitful Soil, to produce in abundance, what might serve for food, rayment and delight; yet for want of improving it by labour, have not one hundredth part of the Conveniencies we enjoy; and a King of a large fruitful Territory there feeds, lodges and is clad worse than a day Labourer in England. (41)

> But there was a natural limit to the amount of perishable goods an individual could claim. If he gathered so much that they rotted in his possession, then he harmed other people and had no right to them. The true accumulation of wealth began with the invention of money, an imperishable means of exchange.

> Yet there are still great Tracts of Ground to be found, which (the Inhabitants thereof not having joyned with the rest of Mankind, in the consent of the use of their common Money)

lie waste, and are more than the People who dwell on it, do, or can make use of, and so still lie in common. (44:21–28)

Not to hide his point, Locke continued immediately to identify these tracts with the "in-land parts of America" (48:21–25). The tribes' land title was limited, he reasoned, not only by their ignorance of agriculture but also by their lack of a means of exchange. Because they did not have the means of storing their accumulated wealth in imperishable form, the land beyond that portion providing for their immediate subsistence, lay "waste," a commons for the use of anyone who brought labor and commerce to improve it.

Furthermore, continued Locke, without money to facilitate the accumulation of property, the Nations of the New World had no incentive to develop more elaborate political structures than temporary elective chiefdoms:

> Thus we see that the Kings of the Indians in America, which is still a Pattern of the first Ages in Asia and Europe, whilst the Inhabitants were too few for the Country, and want of People and Money gave Men [n]o Temptation to enlarge their Possessions of Land, or contend for wider extent of Ground, are little more than Generals of their Armies. (108:1–7)

Convertible Currency

But it is not true to say that North American Indians were ignorant of the idea of imperishable means of exchange. Wampum, carved by Long Island Indians from Quahog shells, served that purpose very well. (Stores near the Poospatuck Indian Reservation in eastern Long Island continued to accept wampum for purchases well into the twentieth century.) In a later passage, Locke shows that he was well aware of wampum, even calling it wampompeke (184:21), a close transliteration of the Algonquin term wampompeag. This reference appears in his chapter "On Conquest," when he describes the strictly arbitrary assignment of value to money:

> These are none of Nature's Goods, they have but a Phantastical imaginary value; Nature has put no such upon them; they are of no more account by her standard, than the Wampompeke

TV Indians © 2005 Frank Salcido

of the Americans to an European Prince, or the silver money of Europe would have been formerly to an American. (184:18–24)

So American Indians do understand the role of money, after all. The difference for Europeans is that they do not have a convertible currency.

There are other indications in the *Second Treatise* that Locke realized that the reality of American tribal life was more sophisticated than his simple stereotype of the hunter-gatherer nomad. "The wild Indian" first appears, or at least appears to appear, as a denizen of the State of Nature, still "a Tenant in common" of the forest which provides him with acorns, apples and venison. His acquisition of property is the most basic; by eating the wild fruits and game, he makes them part of his body, so "that another can no longer have any right" to these natural goods. But this example is too abstract.

Later, citing early Spanish and French Jesuit accounts, Locke offers American Indians as historic examples of the emergence of civil society. He cites the writing of the Spanish Jesuit missionary Jose de Acosta (1539-1600) to answer the objection *"that there are no instances to be found in Story of a Company of Men independent and equal one amongst another, that met together and in this way began and set up a Government"* (100:2–5, Locke's italics).

Locke continues,

> And if Josephus Acosta's word may be taken he tells us that in many parts of America there was no government at all. There are great and apparent Conjectures, says he, that these men, speaking of those of Peru, for a long time had neither Kings nor Common-wealths, but lived in Troops, as they do this day in Florida, the Cheriquanas, those of Bresil, and many other Nations, which have no certain Kings, but as occasion is offered in Peace or War, they choose their Captains as they please. (l.1,c. 25)

Civil Society

This voluntary election of war-chiefs appears several times in Locke's polemic against Sir Robert Filmer's doctrine of the Divine Right of Kings:

These men, 'tis evident, were actually free; and whatever superiority some Politicians now would place in any of them, they themselves claimed it now; but by consent were all equal, till by the same consent they set Rulers over themselves. (101: 6–14, 19–24)

So American Indians are no longer savages in the State of Nature. They are examples of the emergence of civil society. In Central and South America, in fact, they had built advanced urban civilizations, and in the northern forests, they united by consent to choose chiefs as needed. Locke indeed omitted one of the most striking political achievements of the northern Natives, the formation of the Haudenosaunee (Iroquois) Confederation. One doubts he didn't know about it, since it played an important role in British diplomacy when he was in charge of monitoring colonial affairs.

But Locke had a vested interest in ignoring evidence of the political and diplomatic sophistication of the North American tribes, not to mention their extensive settlements and agricultural economy. He was constructing his theory toward a desired result, the appropriation of Indian land.

A later passage confirms this point. In an apparently contradictory argument, Locke expressly repudiated the idea that conquest gave an invader title to land. In a long chapter "On Conquest," he elaborately argued that the victor in a just war could only claim enough property to compensate for the cost of the conflict. Everything else remained the estate of the inhabitants. So far, his argument followed the tradition of Francisco de Vitoria and the other early founders of International Law. But he left a large loophole. "For the Damages of War can scarce amount to the value of any considerable Tract of Land, in any part of the World, where all the Land is possessed, and none lies waste." "Waste" land remained fair game.

Erratic Nations

This doctrine of a right to underused land passed into the emerging body of international law. Emmerich de Vattel (1714-1767), who claimed to be the first self-conscious writer in the new field, incorporated Locke's argument wholesale into his widely read treatise, the *Law of Nations; or Principles of the Law of Nature: Applied to the conduct and*

Affairs of Nations and Sovereigns.[9] Vattel was frequently cited in the Indian law cases of the early nineteenth century. Chief Justice John Marshall himself, along with dissenting Justices Thompson and Story, quoted him in the 1831 case of *Cherokee Nation v. State of Georgia.* The relevant passage is worth reproducing in full, because it makes Locke's purpose crystal clear, and also shows a bad conscience:

> There is another celebrated question, to which the discovery of the new world has principally given rise. It is asked if a nation may lawfully take possession of a part of a vast country, in which there are found none but erratic nations, incapable, by the smallness of their numbers, to people the whole? We have already observed in establishing the obligation to cultivate the earth, that these nations cannot exclusively appropriate to themselves more land than they have occasion for, and which they are unable to settle and cultivate. Their removing their habitations through these immense regions, cannot be taken for a true and legal possession; and the people of Europe, too closely pent up, finding land of which these nations are in no particular want, and of which they make no actual and constant use, may lawfully possess it, and establish colonies there. We have already said, that the earth belongs to the human race in general, and was designed to furnish it with subsistence: if each nation has resolved from the beginning to appropriate to itself a vast country, that the people might live only by hunting, fishing, and wild fruits, our globe would not be sufficient to maintain a tenth part of its present population. People have not then deviated from the views of nature in confining the Indians within narrower limits. However, we cannot help praising the moderation of the English puritans who first settled in New England; who, notwithstanding their being furnished with a charter from their sovereign, purchased of the Indians the land they resolved to cultivate. This laudable example was followed by Mr. William Penn, who planted the colony of quakers in Pennsylvania.[10]

This argument quickly leads to dangerous territory. Indians were not its only victims. The Forty-niners in California used it to justify squatting on the large Spanish land grants; they called it, in mock Latin, the "lex diggerorum."[11] Once the principle extends beyond clearly identifiable "s," it leads to endless lawlessness. What would prevent someone from claiming title to land because he could use it more efficiently than the previous owner? Under this principle, factory farms could claim the land of family farms, and factories could claim the land of farms. This is the spirit of the Supreme Court's decision in *Kelo v. City of New London*, possibly its most controversial ruling in 2004.[12] The court held that the city could condemn private homes by eminent domain so that a private developer could build a commercial project that would produce higher property tax payments.

Mere Occupants

Locke's standard for productive use also appears narrow and short-range in light of subsequent human experience with the degradation of the environment and the onset of rapid global climate change, serious challenges to the idea that industrialization is an unalloyed benefit. What if Spanish ranches, not to mention Indian hunting grounds, were better suited to the climate and soil, say, of the semi-arid West than sod-busting intensive farming? What if conservation of so-called waste land does less damage in the long run than over-exploitation?

Perhaps, a glimpse of these difficulties caused Marshall to shy away from Locke in the seminal 1823 Indian title case *Johnson and Graham's Leasee v. William M'Intosh*.[13] The defendants vigorously pushed Locke's argument, with frequent citations to his *Second Treatise* and to Vattel. But Marshall refused to be drawn in. "We will not enter into the controversy," he wrote, "whether agriculturists, merchants and manufacturers, have a right, on abstract principles, to expel hunters from the territory they possess, or to contract their limits." He fell back on the Doctrine of Discovery, while admitting its absurdity and the injustice of treating the Indians "merely as occupants... incapable of transferring the absolute title to others."[14]

> However this restriction may be opposed to natural right, and to the usage of civilized nations,/ yet, if it be indispensable to that system under which the country has been settled, and be adapted to the actual condition of the two people, it may, perhaps, be supported by reason, and certainly cannot be rejected by Courts of Justice:[15]

Even here, however, the Doctrine of Discovery, stripped of religious pretensions, fell back on the assertion that Europeans were the superior civilization and the Natives were savage nomads.

> Although we do not mean to engage in the defence of those principles which Europeans have applied to Indian title, they may, we think, find some excuse, if not justification, in the character and habits of the people whose rights have been wrested from them...

> [...] the tribes of Indians inhabiting this country were fierce savages, whose occupation was war, and whose subsistence was drawn chiefly from the forest. To leave them in possession of their country, was to leave the country a wilderness...[16]

Today's U.S. Supreme Court

This stereotype was not true even when Marshall wrote, as he was shortly forced to admit in the Cherokee cases. It was certainly not true in the twentieth and twenty-first centuries. Yet, as Williams so damningly shows, it persists in Supreme Court decisions to the present day. The image of the Indian as a primitive nomad occupying undeveloped wastes has become central to American self-justification. Descendants of settlers can assuage any pangs of guilt by contemplating how much more they have produced from the land than did the original inhabitants.

This Lockean argument surfaced again on March 29, 2005, in the eight-to-one ruling in *City of Sherrill v. Oneida Indian Nation*.[17]

Justice Ruth Bader Ginsburg dipped back into nineteenth century precedent to prevent the Oneidas from asserting sovereignty over their reacquired aboriginal territory.

She quoted from the 1892 case *Felix v. Patrick*, rejecting an Indian land claim in Omaha: "[t]hat which was wild land thirty years ago is now intersected by streets, subdivided into blocks and lots, and largely occupied by persons who have bought upon the strength of Patrick's title and have erected buildings of a permanent character."

In the present case, she argued by marshalling another quote, Indian sovereignty had been superceded by "development of every type imaginable." These "pragmatic concerns" boiled down to the Lockean argument that the settlers by their labor had increased the value of what once was "wild land."

The Court found it inconceivable that land under tribal sovereign control could generate far more commercial wealth than land in the hands of the descendants of European settlers.

But this is increasingly the experience across the country. In a number of regions tribal enterprises are the driving force in the local economy and the largest employers. By the principles of John Locke, would not such an economically successful tribe be justified in reclaiming land from the stagnating mainstream society?

▼ ▼ ▼

James Adams is a Senior Historian at the Smithsonian National Museum of the American Indian. He was formerly associate editor of Indian Country Today *and a writer for the* Wall Street Journal.

Notes

1. See John Mohawk, "A Racist Doctrine Ensures Racist Behavior," *Indian Country Today*, vol. 25, no. 42, March 29, 2006; and Lewis Hanke, *Aristotle and the American Indians, A Study in Race Prejudice in the Modern World* (Bloomington, IN: Indiana University Press, 1959). At the great debate at Valladolid before a council summoned by Charles V to determine Spanish policy toward the Indians, Sepulveda presented a distorted version of Aristotle's theory of Natural Slavery. In the original passage in his Politics, Aristotle referred to people lacking the intelligence to provide prudently for themselves, a condition we might describe as severe retardation. It was an implicit rebuke to the institution of slavery as he knew it, where servitude was a result of misfortune in war, and it was not unknown for slaves to be more intelligent and learned than their more militarily robust masters.

2. Robert A. Williams, Jr., *Like a Loaded Weapon, The Rehnquist Court, Indian Rights and the Legal History of Racism in America* (Minneapolis: University of Minnesota Press, 2005), pp. xxi, 47, passim.

3. See, for example, Katy Squadrito, "Locke and the Dispossession of the American Indian," *American Indian Culture and Research Journal*, vol. 20, no. 4 (1996), and her citations on pp. 145–47.

4. In the *Second Treatise*, Locke cites Jose de Acosta's *Historia natural y moral de las Indias*, published in Seville in 1590, and Gabriel Sagard's Canada (1636). Quotations from the both treatises are cited by paragraph and line numbers. Opening quotation is *Second Treatise*, 26:14–15.

5. H. R. Fox Bourne, *The Life of John Locke* (London: Henry King & Co, 1876), reprinted by Thoemmes Press, Bristol, 1992, pp. 238–43.

6. Bourne, *John Locke*, p. 287.

7. Bourne, *John Locke*, p. 241.

8. John Locke, *Two Treatises of Government*, ed. Peter Laslett (New York: New American Library, 1965).

9. Emmerich de Vattel, *The Law of Nations; or, Principles of the Law of Nature: Applied to the Conduct and Affairs of Nations and Sovereigns* (Dublin: printed for Luke White, 1787).

10. de Vattel, *Law of Nations*, pp. 165–66. See also Book II, §97, p. 265, where Vattel defends the rights of "Arabian shepherds" but not the Indians of North America.

11. James Ring Adams, *Secrets of the Tax Revolt* (San Diego: Harcourt Brace Jovanovich, 1984), p. 128, nn. 370–71.

12. *Kelo v. City of New London*, 125 S.Ct. 2655 ().

13. *Johnson and Graham's Leasee v. William M'Intosh*, 21 U.S. 543 (1823).

14. *Johnson*, 21 U.S. 543, p. 588.

15. *Johnson*, 21 U.S. 543, pp. 591–92.

16. *Johnson*, 21 U.S. 543, pp. 589–90.

17. *City of Sherrill v. Oneida Indian Nation*, 125 S.Ct. 1478 ().

Good Indian, Bad Indian

– by Suzan Shown Harjo –

Suzan Shown Harjo speaking at "Hear Our Story: Communications and Contemporary Native Americans," a conference cosponsored by the American Friends Service Committee and the American Indian Policy and Media Initiative in Washington, D.C. in March 2006.

G ood afternoon.
According to the program, my topic is "Old and New Stereotypes."

They're just stereotypes. The old ones are the new ones; the new ones are the old ones.

If you look back in headlines and in news stories from the earliest days of the American press, you find that, whenever they wanted to call us something bad, they called us "Redskins." And the "R" word continues to be that same kind of bad word that's used. Whenever they want to call us something awful, they call us that.

Now, why did they choose that term?

Well, back in history it was referred to the actual practice of skinning Indians. It was the actual practice of providing Indian pelts, Indian skins, as evidence for bounties for Indians killed. When the governors of the colonies put out their proclamations for bounties for Indians, they didn't say, "Just bring me an Indian" or "Tell me how many you killed" or "Bring me a scalp." That wasn't what they said.

They said, "We'll pay eighty cents, sixty cents, forty cents." It was a sliding scale for men, women and children. Now, how did they show it was a man, woman, or child? Through the whole body or through the skin and genitals. That's how that term came about.

Now, that's something that a lot of white folks who are called "Indian experts" dispute today because they haven't found any paper that says, "We're going to start killing Indians in this way and the term is going to derive from that practice of bounty hunting and bounty paying in precisely this way." And if you don't have paper on your side, you can't prove your case.

There's no real regard for oral history, although the courts have shown great deference to Native peoples' oral histories. The Ninth Circuit, for example, was the court that affirmed the Boldt Decision, which affirmed treaty fishing rights in the Pacific Northwest. It showed enormous deference to Indian oral history about fishing, where the fish came from on- and off-reservation, usual and accustomed fishing places, how we used to do it, how we do it now, etc.

But that has changed over time. And you see the same Ninth Circuit Court in the case of the Ancient One, called Kennewick Man, saying, we don't like oral history. We don't think it stands up as much as the written word.

The written word in America has been mostly against Native Peoples, and that's something that we need to understand and to counter. Everyone likes paper. Get paper and replace the paper that you have in your tribes with good paper and keep in mind that words, words, words, are important, important, important.

So I am the person who will be snarky about the title of this conference. We shouldn't use words that diminish the importance of what we are trying to accomplish.

A story is an opinion, but lesser. It's just your version of the truth. When you mean history, and you mean to relate your history, say history. It is another word story that has diminished our authority, like myth and legend, when we mean religious history, when we mean ceremony, when we mean the truth.

Myth is something that is almost a lie. But it's a word that is so associated with Native peoples. Legend is so associated with Native peoples. We don't even skip or run or jump. We roam. Indians are roamers.

We have to change these things that equate us with herds of animals. I don't mind being associated with animals, but it means something when other people look at us as something less than human. It's the opposite of what history instructs.

We're not the ones who would agree to something, who would give something away and then take it back. We're the people who ceded lands and never got them back. But we did that for certain things that are being constantly taken away, and taken away, and taken away; and that has implications for today.

Someone asked a question about the Abramhoff scandal earlier. It comes from this Indian giver, from this less-than, from this colonization, in which we have been stripped of our identities, of our names, of our nationhood, of our personhood, of our citizenship.

We're called members rather than citizens. Our sovereignty is diminished by the language we choose. In that way, we are colonized to trust the white people even though we do not trust them. But we are colonized. We are socialized to have less trust in ourselves, and that's why we abdicate our advocacy to people in the face of evidence that they are doing something negative to us.

We are our own best advocates. So I urge you to not let your advocacy go to someone else, especially at the cost of anything over a thousand bucks. And when you're talking about tens of millions of dollars, that's extraordinary.

For what? For a seat at a restaurant that the guy owned? For a pat on the head?

That is a by-product of the terms of diminution that have been used *about* us, and used *by* us so many times, and used in the press to characterize us to the point where we believe it ourselves.

In the recesses of our psyches, somewhere we think that we are not equal to the Abrahmoffs of the world, we have bought into the lies that have been spread about us, the rumors that have been spread of us, in the American press then and now. We are people who believe in our own victimhood, unfortunately, and who kind of live out that scenario, rather than the people who know how to make war and who know how to make peace and who instruct about honor, who really live and can live honor.

So these things are important to live, not just to think about on Saturdays or learn about in Tuesday classes. But to understand that these words and images about us are directly tied to our future and the way that people treat us.

It's directly tied to the way we give people permission to behave toward us. At some point, if you are being treated badly, you have to stand up, no matter the cost, and say, "You don't get to do that anymore to my children. You cannot do this anymore to my children. Enough is enough."

That is the kind of thing that we need to do over and over and over again until we get it right. And we have to tell the American media, "You don't get to tell these bad stories anymore. We're not the bad people you report in the press."

I was amazed by the *New York Times'* use of stereotypes in their recent series. The *New York Times* is a good paper. But the *New York Times*, when my great chief, the Cheyenne Peace Chief, Black Kettle, was murdered, was massacred by Custer on the orders of Sheridan, the *New York Times* celebrated the death, the killing of Black Kettle, by saying, "it's good that he and his whole ring are done away with. We celebrate this."

That's the *New York Times* of old. The *New York Times* of today has more white glove racism, white glove reporting about the "other." And it's our best paper. It's a wonderful paper. It's the paper of record. But it's been the paper of record about the bad news about us, and reporting us as bad people when we are not, and making our great people something less than we are.

At the same time, what you see happening, and this is so hilarious to me, is that the American media will elevate the people who are pretending to be Native peoples so that some of our most famous Indians are not Indian at all—Ward Churchill and Jimmy Durham and Roxanne Dunbar-Ortiz. All of these people have been totally debunked as Native people, as well as the person who wrote "The Education of Little Tree." They are totally accepted and promoted as the purveyors of knowledge about Native people and as the culture speakers about Native peoples.

And why? Because they're so much like them. They've seen themselves. They haven't seen Indians. They've seen themselves. And they always gravitate to either the good Indians or the non-Indians who are pretending to be Indians, and elevate them, and try to separate the hostiles from the good Indians.

This is something that was done in a formal fashion from 1880 until the mid-1930s under the *Civilization Regulations Act* where you would be declared a hostile, or a troublemaker, or a fomenter of dissent, or a ringleader if you practiced your religion, if you spoke your language, if you didn't behave like a civilized person, which meant Christian, English, short hair, no dancing.

If you danced, this kill order from the *Civilization Regulations Act* could be given to someone else, saying you were not a good Indian. Or if you roamed off the reservation…it actually says, no roaming off the reservation.

If you went to your sacred place to worship and it was off the reservation, if you roamed over that way, you could be declared a hostile and killed.

So it set up this bad Indian– good Indian paradigm that we are still suffering from.

So be very careful about the people you see elevated very, very quickly. Often, they're either the too-good Indians or the non-Indians who are very, very familiar because they aren't Indian in the first instance.

We are people who oftentimes live out our stereotypes and pander to the worst stereotypes about us. Many of our people think there are only two choices. One is the good stereotype of the stoic Indian who is leading the people down the trail of defeat so you have the Indian slumped over the horse.

So that's one stereotype, the end of the trail Indian.

The other stereotype would be the drunk in the gutter.

So one is desirable. The other is undesirable.

Where do you go?

A lot of people don't know that there is a middle ground. That the truth is in the middle. They think they have to be one stereotype or another. I've talked to many Indian young people who actually say, "I didn't know you could be Indian and not drink." That's pretty sad. Fortunately, I've talked to many more who do know the difference. But that's the kind of internalizing of our own oppression and suppression and colonization that can manifest itself so easily.

So don't buy into your own awful headlines. Don't believe the stereotypes and, remember, there's no such thing as a good stereotype. For the Indians, don't be a good Indian. For the non-Indians, pay attention to what the hostiles say.

Suzan Shown Harjo, Cheyenne and Hodulgee Muscogee, is president of the Morning Star Foundation in Washington, D.C. She is a columnist with Indian Country Today, *a poet, and founding co-chairwoman of The Howard Simons Fund for American Indian Journalists. She lives on Capital Hill.*

Blackhorse v. Pro-Football Inc.

*Filed with the Trademark Trial and Appeal Board
of the U.S. Patent and Trademark Office*

In 1992 a lawsuit was filed in the U.S. Trademark Trial and Appeals Board asserting that Pro-Football Inc., the parent company of the Washington Redskins, had repeatedly violated trademark law by licensing names that are disparaging to Native Americans.

The suit filed by Native American leaders in letters, arts and law was a landmark moment in the thirty-year drive to end the use to Native Americans as sports mascots.

Harjo v. Pro-Football Inc., was built on a provision of the U.S. Trademark law which forbids the registration of trademarks which are disparaging, or which hold someone or a group to disrepute or contempt.

The suit was innovative for working not to ban the offensive names and images, but rather to take away its economic value to Pro-Football Inc., by cancelling its trademark. In 1999, the Trademark board ruled in favor of the plaintiffs, who include Suzan Shown Harjo, Raymond D. Apodaca, Vine Deloria, Jr., Norbert Hill, Jr., Mateo Romero, William A. Means and Manley A. Begay, Jr. Pro-Football Inc., is owned by Daniel M. Snyder.

In 2003 a ruling by U.S. District Court Judge Colleen Kollar-Kotelly overturned the earlier decision.

Kollar-Kotelly found that there wasn't enough evidence that the term Redskins was offensive to all Indians, particularly because the trademark had been registered multiple times between 1967, the year of the first trademark registration of the name, and 1990 without complaint. She found that plaintiffs had waited an unreasonably long time to file for cancellation of the trademark. Harjo objected to the ruling in *Indian Country Today,* saying that only one of the plaintiffs was twenty-one years old in 1967, "and Romero wasn't even a toddler."

Still the procedural ruling seemed to derail the case, while substantially failing to acknowledge to the racist and disparaging nature of the sports teams' name.

In August 2006, six young Native Americans filed a backup petition for cancellation of the trademark, which will go forward if *Harjo v. Pro-Football Inc.,* is defeated. Lead plaintiff Amanda Blackhorse, like her fellow plaintiffs, was college age at the time of filing. Their motion for cancellation of the trademark on the Redskins name, related names, stylized lettering and design follows.

–Kara Briggs, Editor

**IN THE UNITED STATES PATENT AND TRADEMARK OFFICE BEFORE THE
TRADEMARK TRIAL AND APPEAL BOARD**

In re Registration No. 1,606,810 (REDSKINETTES)
  Registered July 17, 1990,
Registration No. 1,085,092 (REDSKINS)
  Registered February 7, 1978,
Registration No. 987,127 (THE REDSKINS & DESIGN)
  Registered June 25, 1974,
Registration No. 986,668 (WASHINGTON REDSKINS & DESIGN)
  Registered June 18, 1974,
Registration No. 978,824 (WASHINGTON REDSKINS)
  Registered February 12, 1974,
and Registration No. 836,122 (THE REDSKINS—STYLIZED LETTERS)
  Registered September 26, 1967

Amanda Blackhorse,	)	
Marcus Briggs,	)	
Phillip Gover,	)	
Shquanebin Lone-Bentley,	)	
Jillian Pappan, and	)	
Courtney Tsotigh	)	
	)	
Petitioners,	)	Cancellation No. _____
	)	
v.	)	
	)	
Pro-Football, Inc.	)	
	)	
Registrant.	)	

PETITION FOR CANCELLATION

Petitioners, AMANDA BLACKHORSE, a member of Not in Our Honor, a student

advocacy group aimed at protesting disparaging mascots, an advocate for Indigenous women at

Women's Transitional Care Services, an enrolled member of the Navajo Nation, a federally

recognized Native American tribe, and a Kansas resident; MARCUS BRIGGS, a counselor for

the Indian Youth of America, the President of Sigma Nu Alpha Gamma, the Society of Native

American Gentlemen at the University of Oklahoma, member of Gekakwitha Conference,

member of the American Indian Honor Society, member of the Cultural Affairs committee of the

American Indian Student Association at the University of Oklahoma, President of Campus

Ministry at the University of Oklahoma, recipient of the 2005 Big 12 American Indian

Leadership Award, recipient of the 2002 American Indian Leadership Award for the State of

Florida, a member of the Muscogee Nation of Florida tribe (a son of the Wind Clan), and a

Florida resident; PHILLIP GOVER, former head of the Native American Student Union at the

University of Virginia, an enrolled member of the Paiute Indian Tribe of Utah, a federally

recognized Native American tribe, and a Virginia resident; SHQUANEBIN LONE-BENTLEY, a

member of the National Congress of American Indians, a member of United South and Eastern

Tribes, a member of the American Indian Society, an enrolled member of the Tonawanda Band

of the Seneca Nation, a federally recognized Native American tribe, and a Virginia resident;

JILLIAN PAPPAN, a member of the Native American Journalists Association, a member of the

Omaha Tribe of Macy, Nebraska, a federally recognized Native American tribe, and an Iowa

resident; and COURTNEY TSOTIGH, an Oklahoma City University student, a board member of

the General Commission on Religion and Race, a registered member of the Kiowa Tribe of

Oklahoma, a federally recognized Native American tribe, and an Oklahoma resident (collectively

hereinafter, "Petitioners"), in their capacity as Native American persons and enrolled members of

Native American tribes, believe that they have been, are, and/or will be damaged by U.S.

Registration Nos. 1,606,810; 1,085,092; 987,127; 986,668; 978,824 and 836,122 (collectively,

the "Registrations"), registered in the name of Pro-Football, Inc. (hereinafter "Registrant"), a

Maryland corporation, having a place of business at 21300 Redskin Park Drive, Ashburn,

Virginia 22011, and hereby petition to cancel said registrations.

In 1999, the Trademark Trial and Appeal Board (the "Board") ruled on a similar Petition

to Cancel the Registrations brought by a different group of Native American petitioners. In

Harjo v. Pro-Football, Inc., 50 U.S.P.Q.2d 1705 (T.T.A.B. 1999), the Board cancelled the

DC\573145\5

– 52 –

registrations after it examined the record, including extensive evidence concerning the history of use and perception of the word "Redskin," and concluded that the term "Redskin" was disparaging.

Pro-Football appealed the decision to the United States District Court for the District of Columbia. The District Court reversed the Board's ruling, holding that the Board should have deemed the *Harjo* petitioners' claim barred by laches, and that, alternatively, the Board's disparagement finding was unsupported by substantial evidence. *Pro-Football, Inc. v. Harjo*, 284 F. Supp.2d 96 (D.D.C. 2003).

The Native Americans, in turn, appealed the District Court's decision to the United States Court of Appeals for the District of Columbia Circuit ("D.C. Circuit Court of Appeals"). The D.C. Circuit Court of Appeals remanded the case back to the District Court on the ground that one of the original petitioners, Mateo Romero, was only one year old when the first of the six Registrations issued. Because the clock on laches only begins to run when individual reaches the age of majority, the D.C. Circuit Court of Appeals explained that Mateo Romero's claim may not be barred by laches. *Pro-Football, Inc. v. Harjo*, 75 U.S.P.Q.2d 1525 (D.C. Cir. 2005). The case has been remanded by the D. C. Circuit Court of Appeals and is now pending in District Court.

Each of the Petitioners bringing this Petition to Cancel have only just recently reached the age of majority, the age from which the D.C. Circuit Court of Appeals has determined that laches begins to run. Because Petitioners in this action are bringing a claim that is very similar to the one that was before the Board in the *Harjo* case, they plan to rely on a significant portion of the evidence present in the *Harjo* record for proving their case, pursuant to 37 CFR § 2.122(f).

The grounds for cancellation are as follows:

1. The term "REDSKIN" or an abbreviation of that term appears in each of the above-identified registered marks. The term "REDSKIN" was and is a pejorative, derogatory, denigrating, offensive, scandalous, contemptuous, disreputable, disparaging, and racist designation for a Native American person. The marks identified in U.S. Registration Nos. 986,668 and 987,127 also include additional matter that in the context used by Registrant, is offensive, disparaging, and scandalous. The Registrant's use of each mark identified in the six above registrations offends Petitioners, and other Native Americans, causing them to be damaged by the continued registration of the marks.

2. Registrant's six above-identified federally registered marks consist of or comprise matter that disparages Native American persons, and brings them into contempt, ridicule, and disrepute, in violation of Section 2(a) of the Lanham Act, 15 U.S.C. § 1052(a).

WHEREFORE, Petitioners believe that they have been, are, and/or will be damaged by said registrations and pray that each of them be cancelled.

A check in the sum of the $1800.00 covering the government filing fee for this Petition is enclosed. If for any reason there is no check attached hereto or the amount is insufficient, please charge any fee or insufficiency to this firm's account No. DA 500573.

Respectfully submitted,

Date: August 11, 2006   By: _____

Philip J. Mause
Amy E. Carroll
Drinker Biddle & Reath LLP
1500 K Street, N.W., Suite 1100
Washington, D.C. 20005-1209
Phone: (202) 842-8889; Fax: (202) 842-8465

Attorneys for Petitioners

Manifest Media:
Public Perception around Wounded Knee, 1890

– By Robert W. Venables –

O n December 29, 1890, at Wounded Knee, South Dakota, more than two hundred Lakotas were massacred by the Seventh Cavalry. Wounded Knee marked the conquest of a continent that had begun in 1492 in the bright daylight of the Caribbean and ended as snow and darkness blanketed the slaughtered Lakota men, women and children. But Wounded Knee was also a major assault on an American Indian religion, a religion known in English as "The Ghost Dance." In fact, the overwhelming cruelty of the slaughter was an assault on all American Indian religions, emphasizing that American Indian spirituality had no place in the new order of the United States. Officially sanctioned oppression of Indian religions would not officially end until 1934, when President Franklin D. Roosevelt's administration ended direct U.S. government oppression of American Indian religions.

Religious Oppression

At the core of the Ghost Dance are the teachings revealed by spiritual forces about 1889 to a Paiute living in Nevada, Wovoka ("The Cutter," c.1856-1932). Each Indian nation named the new movement in its own national language. For example, the Paiute name for the Ghost Dance is "Nänigükwa" ("dance in a circle"), while the Lakota (Sioux) term is "Wana'ghi wa'chipi" ("spirit dance"). The "Ghost

Dance" is actually a complex philosophy expressed in ceremony by a series of dances. The philosophy and the dances prepare followers for a rebalancing of a world that had been nearly destroyed by the expansion of the United States. The rebalance would be carried out by spiritual forces and would include the return from the dead of all of the Indian people's relatives, including both human relatives and other relatives such as buffalo.

Wovoka's teachings extended earlier Indian religious traditions and incorporated a few Christian concepts as well. The teachings stressed that people must live peacefully, ethically and cooperatively. Continuing revelations occurred among the religious leaders of different Indian nations. Thus local variations of the Ghost Dance were manifested in philosophy, dance, music and art. The most notable variations concerned the white race. Some Ghost Dance adherents believed that the rebalanced new world would have to include the white invaders who were now the Indians' neighbors. But others believed that the whites would have to disappear in order for a rebalancing to occur, and that this disappearance might be hastened by a renewed Indian resistance to United States expansion. Many also believed that their ceremonial shirts and dresses made them invulnerable to bullets.

Because this religious movement was feared by the United States government as a possible focal point for Indian resistance, tensions on the frontier increased. The result was the massacre at Wounded Knee. Of the 350 Lakotas there, at least two hundred were killed directly, and about one hundred more died later of wounds and exposure. About thirty-two white soldiers and one of the army's Indian scouts were killed. When Wovoka heard what had happened, he was shocked and dismayed. He believed that his teachings had been misunderstood by leaders of both the Lakotas and the Americans. But the Ghost Dance religion has survived down to the present day, continuing an impressive Indian liturgy of theology, music, dance and art, all affirming faith in the renewal of the world.

The Vanishing Race

The attitudes that led both American citizens and Lakotas to Wounded Knee are complex. Among non-Indians, the America of 1890 was cruel not simply on the frontier. That same year, Jacob A. Riis published "How the Other Half Lives: Studies Among the Tenements of New York," a scathing indictment of the horrific living conditions of American immigrants and the working class in general (Riis, 1890). In this context of the culture of the United States, it is not surprising that often-used American labels to describe Indians were "Vanishing Americans" and the "Vanishing Race." But while these terms were common among American citizens, "vanishing" meant different things to different citizens. Some thought that Indians would be exterminated entirely, while others saw Indians as vanishing into the American population through intermarriage and assimilation (Dixon, 1975). The media reinforced the view that Indians and their cultures were primitive and would either disappear or be assimilated. In *Harper's Weekly* during the 1870s and 1880s, the famous political cartoonist Thomas Nast portrayed Indians either as inferiors or as brutal savages, reflecting a Darwinian view of humanity's evolution. For example, in 1878 one of his cartoons portrays Indians riding away from a burning settler's cabin. Two wounded white men, as well as a dead man, woman, and child, also white, are near the cabin. A caricature of the Secretary of the Interior, Carl Schurz, lectures one of the wounded on the efforts of the government to "civilize" the Indians. The cartoon is entitled "Patience Until the Indian is Civilized—So to Speak" (Nast, 1878). However, Nast was not without a sense of irony when another of his cartoons, dated February 8, 1879, portrayed a stereotypical black man lounging on a cotton bale; a Chinese looking at a wall with posters calling for an end to Chinese immigration; and a grumpy Indian warrior who is looking at the same posters. As captioned by Nast: "RED GENTLEMAN TO YELLOW GENTLEMAN. 'Pale face 'fraid you crowd him out, as he did me" (Nast, 1879).

American tourists in the "Wild West" could purchase souvenir photographs such an 1890 print of three pleasantly-smiling Lakota young men who are wearing trousers and buttoned shirts. They are comfortably seated beneath a tree and clearly do not realize that their portraits will be used to mock them. When this photograph was made, Indians were regarded as dependents, because U.S. law defined Indians as similar to "wards" of the United States. And although treaties guaranteed the Lakotas and other Indians monthly rations of meat and other foods in exchange for land transfers—the equivalent of stock dividends—rations were regarded by many U.S. citizens as undeserved welfare. This particular photograph was offered to the tourists by the photographer G.C.H. Grabill. Numbered photograph 3561, the prominent label on the front of the photo reads,

> "Three of Uncle Sam's Pets. We get rations every 29 days. Our pulse is good. Expressive medium. We put in 60 minutes each hour in our present attitude. Photo and copyright by Grabill, '90" (Weisberger, 1971).

Grabill also took photographs in August 1890 of the very Lakotas slaughtered at Wounded Knee.

An Outspoken Sentiment

Not all U.S. citizens saw Indians in negative stereotypes, however. In 1881, less than a decade before Wounded Knee, Helen Hunt Jackson published the scathing indictment of U.S. government Indian policies entitled *Century of Dishonor*. A revised edition was published in 1885:

> Colorado is as greedy and unjust in 1880 as was Georgia in 1830, and Ohio in 1795; and the United States government breaks promises now as deftly as then, and with an added ingenuity from long practice....

> The testimony of some of the highest military officers of the United States is on record to the effect that, in our Indian wars, almost without exception, the first aggressions have been made by the white man.... In addition to the class of robbers and outlaws who find impunity in their nefarious pursuits on the frontiers, there is a large class of professedly reputable men who use every means in their power to bring on Indian wars for the sake of profit to be realized from the presence of troops and the expenditure of government funds in their midst.

> The history of the United States government's repeated violations of faith with the Indians thus convicts us, as a nation....

> There is but one hope of righting this wrong. It lies in appeal to the heart and conscience of the American people. What the people demand, Congress will do. It has been—our shame be it spoken—at the demand of parts of the people that all these wrongs have been committed, these treaties broken, these

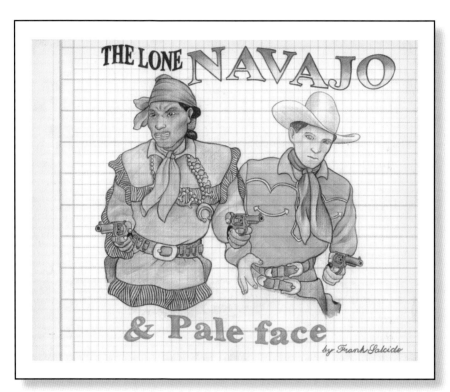

The Lone Navajo & Pale Face © 2002 Frank Salcido

robberies done, by the government....

The only thing that can stay this is a mighty outspoken sentiment and purpose of the great body of the people. (Jackson 1995, 29-30).

That "outspoken sentiment" was in fact a paradox, because that segment of the American public that was sympathetic to Indians, including Helen Hunt Jackson, also believed that Indian religions and customs must inevitably give way to Christianity and western values of government, land, and other social constructs.

Realizing the Gravity

Partially in response to Jackson's book, the United States Congress passed the *Dawes Act* in 1887. The act intended to break up the communal land bases of Indian nations and divide these lands in to small farms and ranches, forcing Indian people to assimilate non-tribal white ways. Before the *Dawes Act* was passed in 1887, white policy towards American Indians had been often been premised as "them or us." After 1887, it was clearly "them into us." Indians saw the period following the *Dawes Act* as one of terrible chaos, as their national ways of life were rent by conquest, Congressional legislation, and their own inability to find their own solutions because their nations were divided among those who wanted to accept assimilation and those who wanted to continue traditional religions, governments and societies.

In the meantime, some adherents of the Ghost Dance believed that their new faith would give Indian nations the power to drive the whites away by force, and would even protect believers from the bullets and shells of the U.S. army. This dramatically altered Wovoka's message. On November 13, 1890, President Benjamin Harrison, Republican, ordered the U.S. Army to be prepared for war. In the midst of this crisis, Lakotas under Rocky Bear arrived at Pine Ridge. They had just returned from Europe where they had performed as part of Buffalo Bill's Wild West Show. Accompanying them was a reporter for the *Omaha Bee*, C.H. Cressey. On November 20, the *Omaha Bee* reported how Cressey believed that these Lakotas,

Seem to a certain extent to realize the gravity of the situation, and it is believed they will do much toward restoring quiet.

Several of the party had received letters from their friends at Pine Ridge speaking of the Christ and Messiah craze [the Ghost Dance] just before they sailed from Europe. (Jensen et al. 1991, 28)

Assassinating Sitting Bull

But on December 1, the crisis still seemed intense and President Harrison ordered the army to "take every possible precaution to prevent an Indian outbreak, and to suppress it promptly if it comes" ((Jensen et al. 1991, 31). The army issued orders to arrest Sitting Bull of the Hunkpapa Lakota, the leader most likely to be able to lead any pan-Indian effort. Such an arrest would have been illegal if attempted on a white leader. Among many things, this order to arrest Sitting Bull indicated that the United States was willing to use old methods of conquest. Ironically, at this same time, the *Dawes Act* was being promoted among Indian people on the premise that the United States possessed superior political and cultural values.

There is strong evidence that Sitting Bull would have preferred a continuation of traditional faith as expressed in the Sun Dance rather than the new Ghost Dance. But the United States did not consider this. At dawn on December 15, 1890, at least thirty-nine Lakota police and four other Lakota volunteers surrounded Sitting Bull's cabin on the Standing Rock Reservation in South Dakota. A few escorted him outside. One of Sitting Bull's followers fired his rifle at the Indian police lieutenant. As he fell, he fired his revolver into Sitting Bull's chest. At the same time, another policeman shot the chief in the head. The two shots instantly killed Sitting Bull. In the bloody skirmish which followed, the Indian police had to take cover in Sitting Bull's cabin to hold off angry warriors. Finally the cavalry rescued them.

We Cannot Regret Their Extermination

At least six press correspondents were at Pine Ridge at this time: Buckskin Jack Kelly of the *Lincoln Journal* (N.E.), C.H. Cressey of the *Omaha Bee* (N.E.) , Carl Smith of the *Omaha Herald*, Charles Seymour of the *Chicago Herald*, Warren K. Moorehead of the *Philadelphia Press*, Charles Allen of the *New York Herald*, and reporters for the *Chicago*

Inter-Ocean, the *Chicago Tribune*, and the Associated Press. But it is the editorial page of the *Aberdeen (SD) Saturday Pioneer* that best reveals the attitude of the frontier newspapers and their readers. On December 20, 1890, the editor offered the following commentary:

> Sitting Bull, the most renowned Sioux of modern history, is dead.
>
> He was not a Chief, but without Kingly lineage he arose from a lowly position to the greatest Medicine Man of his time, by virtue of his shrewdness and daring.
>
> He was an Indian with a white man's spirit of hatred and revenge for those who had wronged him and his. In his day he saw his son and his tribe gradually driven from their posessions [sic] forced to give up their old hunting grounds and espouse the hard working and uncongenial avocations of the whites. And these, his conquerors, were marked in their dealings with his people by selfishness, falsehood and treachery. What wonder that his wild nature, untamed by years of subjection, should still revolt? What wonder that a fiery rage still burned within his breast and that he should seek every opportunity of obtaining vengeance upon his natural enemies.
>
> The proud spirit of the original owners of these vast prairies, inherited through centuries of fierce and bloody wars for their possession, lingered last in the bosom of Sitting Bull. With his fall the nobility of the Redskin is extinguished, and what few are left are a pack of whining curs who lick the hand that smites them. The Whites, by law of conquest, by justice of civilization, are masters of the American continent, and the best safety of the frontier settlers will be secured by the total annihilation of the few remaining Indians. Why not annihilation? Their glory has fled, their spirit broken, their manhood effaced; better that they should die than live the miserable wretches that they are. History would forget these latter despicable beings, and speak, in latter ages of the glory of these grand Kings of the forest and plain that Cooper loved to heroism [sic].
>
> We cannot honestly regret their extermination, but we can at least do justice to the manly characteristics posessed [sic],

according to their lights and education, by the early Redskin of America. (*Aberdeen Saturday Pioneer*, 1890)

Having called for the Indians "extermination," the editor continued, with just a graphic line separating his call for genocide from his next item. Since this weekly paper was issued on December 20, Christmas was just five days away and the holiday would occur before the next weekly issue was published. And so the editor wrote the following:

> It is on Christmas day that the Nativity of Christ is observed....
>
> The Kris Kringle or, Santa Claus, is a relic of the ancient Yule Feast, so that the festival of Christmas is a curious mingling of ancient heathen and Christian customs, albeit a very pleasing and satisfactory celebration to the people of today.
>
> With this issue it is a pleasant duty to us to wish all our readers a Merry Christmas. (*Aberdeen Saturday Pioneer*, 1890).

Ten years later, the editor quoted above, L. Frank Baum, would write *The Wizard of Oz*, one of the most famous books in American literature.

The Seventh Cavalry

On December 28, in the midst of all these tensions, the Seventh Cavalry brought 350 Lakotas to a campsite at Wounded Knee Creek, South Dakota, where they were to be disarmed. Led by Big Foot, the band had tried to escape into the Bad Lands where a resistance movement might have been possible, but the cavalry had caught up with them. This was not just any cavalry. This was the Seventh, carrying on the "tradition" of George Armstrong Custer who had been defeated by the Lakotas and the Cheyennes at the Little Big Horn back in 1876. This defeat was seared into the American mind in no small measure because it occurred during the Centennial year of the Declaration of Independence. The image of the Indian as a savage warrior was perpetuated by lithographs of the Custer battle of 1876, especially a version of Cassily Adams' "Custer's Last Stand" which was distributed to taverns across the country by Anheuser-Busch to promote their beer sales.

No less a poet than Walt Whitman, today deservedly known for his observations of mankind, wrote a paean to Custer after the battle. Whitman's open homosexuality should have made him sensitive to the plight of another oppressed people. But Whitman's pride in the American experiment meant that this great poet was as absorbed by his culture as was L. Frank Baum, who as the editor penned the racist editorial quoted above but who was obviously also capable of such sensitivity that he could later write *The Wizard of Oz*. Whitman's sense of nationalist identity had been made even stronger by his earlier service as a nurse during the Civil War. Whitman's admiration for Union heroes included Custer, for Custer had served the Union cause courageously. Even knowing that Whitman was of course a product of his era, the tone of his poem is still unexpected, especially Whitman's concluding lines transforming Custer into a Christ-like martyr.

From Far Dakota's Canons
June 25, 1876
By Walt Whitman

> From far Dakota's cañons,
> Lands of the wild ravine, the dusky Sioux, the
>   lonesome stretch, the silence,
> Haply to-day a mournful wail, haply a trumpet-note
>   for heroes.
>
> The battle bulletin,
> The Indian ambuscade, the craft, the fatal
>   environment,
> The cavalry companies fighting to the last in sternest
>   heroism,
> In the midst of their little circle, with their slaughter'd
>   horses for breast-works,
> The fall of Custer and all his officers and men.
>
> Continues yet the old, old legend of our race,
> The loftiest of life upheld by death,
> The ancient banner perfectly maintain'd,
> O lesson opportune, O how I welcome thee!

As sitting in dark days,
Lone, sulky, through the times thick murk looking in
    vain for light, for hope,
From unsuspected parts a fierce and momentary
    proof,
(The sun there at the centre though concealed,
Electric life forever at the centre,)
Breaks forth a lightning flash.

Thou of the tawny flowing hair in battle,
I erstwhile saw, with erect head, pressing ever in front,
bearing a bright sword in thy hand,
Now ending well in death the splendid fever of thy
    deeds,
(I bring no dirge for it or thee, I bring a glad
    triumphal sonnet,)
Desperate and glorious, aye in defeat most desperate,
    most glorious,
After thy many battles in which never yielding up a
    gun or a color,
Leaving behind thee a memory sweet to soldiers,
Thou yieldest up thyself.

(Miller 1959, 335)

Two-Hundred And Thirty Women and Children

Thus the momentum that the Seventh Cavalry brought to Wounded Knee in 1890 was not just of United States' history but of United States' art and culture. All this weighted the odds heavily against the desperate Lakotas of Big Foot's band. In fact all the Lakotas had ample reasons to be discontented. The U.S. government had reduced the rations guaranteed as payment for previous land cessions. Diseases had also ravaged the Lakotas. Any hope among Big Foot's band lay primarily in the sacred promises held out by the Ghost Dance.

Big Foot's followers included 230 women and children and 120 men, of whom perhaps 106 were warriors, the others being old men. A total of 470 troops and thirty scouts surrounded them. From a hill, the military trained four Hotchkiss rapid-fire artillery guns on the Lakota camp.

On the morning of December 29, the warriors were assembled in an area adjacent to the Indian camp, separated from their women and children who remained among the teepees. Some soldiers had been ordered to confiscate all the Lakota weapons, including their Winchester rifles. Troopers went among the women and children in the camp, searching for weapons. Others confronted the warriors. The rifles were important possessions, but more importantly the Lakotas feared that they would be killed if they gave up their only means of protection. A medicine man, Yellow Bird, exhorted the warriors to resist. The sanctified "ghost shirts" which they wore as adherents of the Ghost Dance religion would, he assured them, protect them from bullets. One account states that a Lakota named Black Coyote angrily shouted that he had bought his rifle at great expense and would not turn it over without being paid for it. Another account notes that a deaf Lakota did not understand the command to give up his rifle. And perhaps it was a nervous soldier, but it is clear that someone suddenly fired a rifle. In response, soldiers and warriors fired at each other almost simultaneously. The soldiers' volley was more concentrated and effective. Suddenly the Hotchkiss guns on the ridge above opened fire, its exploding shells striking at the rate of up to fifty per minute, not just killing the warriors but also striking down soldiers who were nearby or among the Indians.

The Hotchkiss Guns

The Hotchkiss guns also fired into that part of the camp where the women and children were. Some warriors joined their wives, children and elderly relatives, intending to protect them. They succeeded only in drawing more Hotchkiss and rifle fire, which wiped out entire families. A few women, separated from the warriors, fought back on their own with rifles. Many if not most of the women and children who were killed were clearly apart from the warriors when they died. Even those women and children who could escape from the center of the carnage were pursued as far as two miles to be butchered by the troopers of the Seventh. Within minutes, at least two hundred Indians lay dead—over half were women and children. Twenty-five soldiers died and thirty were wounded, a few of these had been killed or wounded by the Hotchkiss guns or rifles of their fellow soldiers who had fired indiscriminately during those horrible minutes.

Many whites, settlers and soldiers alike, called Wounded Knee a great battle and a victory. The United States government issued twenty-eight Congressional Medals of Honor to commemorate the actions of white soldiers at Wounded Knee. In a ballad that became popular throughout the west, Private W.H. Prather described what he did not participate in but clearly would like to have. The last verse of the chorus extols,

> E battery of the 1st stood by and did their duty well,
> For every time the Hotchkiss barked they say a hostile
> fell.
> Some Indian soldiers chipped in too and helped to
> quell the fray,
> And now the campaign's ended and the soldiers
> marched away.
> So all have done their share, you see, whether it was
> thick or thin,
> And all helped break the ghost dance up and drive the
> hostiles in.
>
> (Prather 1896)

Private Prather was black, a "Buffalo Soldier" in the black Ninth Cavalry Regiment, one of the units which was intended, if necessary, to support the other troops at Wounded Knee.

Nobody Knew What Was Going On

An Indian point of view was expressed by the Oglala Lakota Black Elk. Decades later he had his close white friend, the poet John G. Neihardt, transcribe what Black Elk had learned from survivors and what he remembered himself. Black Elk, through the words of this poet, recalled some of the events which followed the initial volley of gunfire:

> Then suddenly nobody knew what was happening, except that the soldiers were all shooting and the wagon-guns [Hotchkiss guns] began going off right in among the people.

> Many were shot down right there. The women and children

ran into the gulch and up west, dropping all the time, for the soldiers shot them as they ran. There were only about a hundred warriors and there were nearly five hundred soldiers. The warriors rushed to where they had piled their guns and knives. They fought soldiers with only their hands until they got their guns.

Dog Chief saw Yellow Bird run into a teepee with his gun, and from there he killed soldiers until the tepee caught fire. Then he died full of bullets.

It was a good winter day when all this happened. The sun was shining.

But after the soldiers marched away from their dirty work, a heavy snow began to fall. The wind came up in the night. There was a big blizzard, and it grew very cold. The snow drifted deep in the crooked gulch, and it was one long grave of butchered women and children and babies, who had never done any harm and were only trying to run away.

(Neihardt 1932)

A Tiny Baby Girl

On New Year's Day, 1891, a detachment of troops, American civilians and Lakotas made their way from the Pine Ridge agency to Wounded Knee. A long trench was dug in the frigid ground. Into this mass grave were piled the frozen, contorted bodies of the Lakotas. About eighty-five Lakotas and a few whites had come with the troops to search for survivors. They found a few people still alive even though they had been exposed for two days in the blizzard. Most of these died soon afterwards, but one who lived was a tiny baby girl, less than a year old. Her dead mother, who had been hit by two bullets, lay next to her. On the baby's head was a small buckskin cap, and on the cap, in bright beadwork, was an embroidered American flag. She was named by the Lakota survivors as Zintkala Nuni (also spelled Zitkala-noni), the "Lost Bird." The little girl was adopted by a white officer, General Leonard Wright Colby, and his wife Clara. She was renamed Marguerite Elizabeth, but her stepmother continued to call her Zintka or Zinkala. As Zintka matured, Leonard Colby evidently molested her. Despite her best efforts to find happiness, she was beset with continual personal tragedies. Zintkala Nuni died in California at the early age of twenty-nine in 1920 of influenza and flu, possibly complicated by syphilis, during what would become known as the worst epidemic in United States history (Flood, 1995).

Buffalo Bill's Wild West Show

After Wounded Knee, U. S. military forces massed to choke the life from the Ghost Dance movement. One by one, various groups and bands of Lakotas submitted to U. S. authority. On January 15, 1891, the surrender of a major Lakota Ghost Dance leader, Kicking Bear, marked the end of the movement's outward militancy. Kicking Bear was shipped to Fort Sheridan in Illinois along with other prisoners of war. But by the end of March, Kicking Bear was preparing to embark on another campaign. Soon he and other Indians were mounted on their ponies and galloping into battle in Buffalo Bill Cody's Wild West Show. Buffalo Bill had arranged with the army to recruit the Indians for his upcoming European tour. Crossing the Atlantic, Kicking Bear helped make the Wild West Show a smash hit. For Kicking Bear, show business meant survival.

Kicking Bear and the other Lakotas who joined Buffalo Bill's Wild West Show were only the most recent Indians enlisted by Cody since he had begun staging his spectaculars in 1883. In 1885, even the great leader Sitting Bull had joined the troupe, although he declined a tour to Europe. The degree to which the bonneted horsemen in war paint encouraged the non-Indian audiences to begin to appreciate Indian cultures and how much they pandered to the audiences' desire to see vestiges of the "savage" frontier remains debatable.

But one impact of Cody's Wild West Show both in America and abroad is clear. After 1900, Indians of the Plains cultures, with headdresses and teepees, increasingly became symbolic of all Indians. This in turn led many Indians who did not come from cultures with Plains accoutrements to adopt them so that non-Indians would more readily identify them as "Indians." The Plains image became so pervasive in the non-Indian mind that Indians such as the Cherokees and the Iroquois whose ancestors never wore the Plains' full-feathered and sweeping war bonnets took to wearing them to emphasize their Indian identity to non-Indians. Thus in more than just economic, political and social ways, Indians often became what whites wanted them to appear to be.

Separatism or Assimilation

Individual survival was achieved along a spectrum from Indian nationalism or separatism to assimilation. Kicking Bear and Indians like him were at one end of this survival spectrum, attempting to revive the vigor of Indian societies through the Ghost Dance and then, when their revivalism collapsed, selling their cultural remnants to the eager audiences at Buffalo Bill's Wild West Shows. The circumstances that combined to bring about the tragedy at Wounded Knee and the reduction of Kicking Bear from major disciple to major attraction also involved a Sioux Indian living towards the other end of the spectrum.

Dr. Charles Eastman was a Dakota who had completely met the requirements of the American culture as a trained medical doctor and tried, just as Kicking Bear had tried, to help his people according to his best insights and abilities. Dr. Eastman's mother was Mary Nancy Eastman, the daughter of a Sioux mother and Captain Seth Eastman, a white soldier who was also one of America's most significant artists. Dr. Eastman's father, Many Lightnings, had been converted to Christianity while a prisoner of war following the United States war against the Dakotas in Minnesota in 1862.

From the Santee Indian School run by missionaries in Nebraska, Charles Eastman went to Beloit College, Knox College, and eventually graduated on an Indian scholarship from Dartmouth. In 1890, he received his MD at Boston University and in October of that year took up the government-salaried position of resident physician at the Pine Ridge Sioux agency, South Dakota. On Christmas Day, 1890, Eastman and Elaine Goodale, a New England-born schoolteacher at Pine Ridge who spoke Sioux fluently, announced their engagement.

"Three days later," Eastman recalled…

> We learned that Big Foot's band of ghost dancers from the Cheyenne River reservation north of us was approaching the agency, and that Major Whiteside was in command of troops with orders to intercept them:

Late that afternoon, The Seventh Cavalry under Colonel Forsythe was called to the saddle and rode off toward Wounded Knee creek, eighteen miles away…

The morning of December 29, was sunny and pleasant. We were straining our ears toward Wounded Knee, and about the middle of the forenoon we distinctly heard the reports of the Hotchkiss guns…"

(Eastman 1916, 106–7)

Straining Our Ears

In two hours, the agency received the first reports of Wounded Knee. Eastman tried to go immediately to the site and aid any wounded not brought back to the agency. But the army and the blizzard combined to prevent him from going until three days later, when the storm cleared. Eastman, about eighty-five Lakotas, ten to fifteen white civilians, and a detachment of troops went to Wounded Knee to bury the dead and search for any survivors. A photographer and a number of news reporters also went along. Eastman, who at this point believed that Wounded Knee had been a battle, came upon evidence even before he reached the site that it had been a massacre. Fifteen years later, he remembered what he saw:

Fully three miles from the scene of the massacre we found the body of a woman completely covered with a blanket of snow, and from this point on we found them scattered along as they had been relentlessly hunted down and slaughtered while fleeing for their lives. Some of our people discovered relatives or friends among the dead, and there was so much wailing and mourning. When we reached the spot where the Indian camp had stood, among the fragments of burned tents and other belongings we saw the frozen bodies lying close together or piled one upon another. I counted eighty bodies of men who had been in the council [discussing surrender term] and who were almost as helpless as the women and babes when the deadly fire began, for nearly all their guns had been taken from them. A reckless and desperate young Indian [had] fired the first shot when the search for weapons was well under way, and immediately the troops opened fire from all sides, killing not only unarmed men, women, and children, but their own comrades who stood opposite them, for the camp was entirely surrounded. It took all my nerve to keep my composure in the face of this spectacle, and of the excitement and grief of my Indian companions, nearly every one of whom was crying aloud or singing his death song. The white men became very nervous, but I set them to examining and uncovering every body to see if one were living. Although they had been lying untended in the snow and cold for two days and nights, a number had survived. Among them I found a baby of about a year-old warmly wrapped and entirely unhurt. I brought her in and she was afterward adopted and educated by an Army officer [this was Zinkala Nuni, the child found with the buckskin cap embroidered with a beaded American flag upon it and later adopted by General Colby]. One man who was severely wounded begged me to fill his pipe. When we brought him into the chapel [at Pine Ridge, where it was used as a hospital] he was welcomed by his wife and daughters with cries of joy, but he died a day or two later.

Under a wagon I discovered an old woman, totally blind and entirely helpless. A few had managed to crawl away to some place of shelter...

All of this was a severe ordeal for one who had so lately put all his faith in the Christian love and lofty ideals of the white man. Yet I passed no hasty judgment, and was thankful that I might be of some small service and relieve even a small part of the suffering. An appeal published in a Boston paper brought us liberal supplies of much needed clothing, and linen for dressings...."

(Eastman 1916, 111–14)

A "Fair" Fight

The American public learned of Wounded Knee through various newspaper accounts and illustrations. One of the most memorable of these was an engraving published by *Harper's Weekly* on January 24, 1891. The engraving, entitled "The Opening of the Fight at

Wounded Knee," features dismounted Seventh Cavalry soldiers firing into Lakotas who stand perhaps twenty paces from the soldiers. The engraving puts the viewer into the action, for the perspective places the reader directly behind the soldiers as they fire into the vague mass of Indians, only a few of whom have clearly defined faces, with one wearing the obligatory Plains headdress.

The artist was the already famous Frederick Remington who based this work on the soldiers' accounts. Although the viewer cannot see whether Lakotas are suffering casualties, the impression of engraving is one of an intense combat in the first moments of the fight rather than the outright slaughter that began within a few minutes of this opening round of gunfire. Thus the impression the American public gains from this engraving is one of a "fair" fight, not of a massacre. Of the ten soldiers who figure prominently in the foreground, only five are unscathed. Three lie wounded on the ground; one is already dead and lies splayed on the ground; and one soldier is reeling backwards, struck by an unseen Lakota's bullet.

On January 3, 1891, the *Aberdeen (SD) Saturday Pioneer* went to press again. The editor, L. Frank Baum, summarized his newspaper's view of the meaning of Wounded Knee:

> The peculiar policy of the government in employing so weak and vacillating a person as General [Nelson A.] Miles to look after the uneasy Indians, has resulted in a terrible loss of blood to our soldiers, and a battle which, at its best, is a disgrace to the war department. There has been plenty of time for prompt and decisive measures, the employment of which would have prevented this disaster.

> The Pioneer has before declared that our only safety depends upon the total extermination [sic] of the Indians. Having wronged them for centuries we had better, in order to protect our civilization, follow it up by one more wrong and wipe these untamed and untamable creatures from the face of the earth. In this lies future safety for our settlers and the soldiers who are under incompetent commands. Otherwise, we may expect future years to be as full of trouble with the redskins as those have been in the past.

[A graphic line appears at this point.]

> An eastern contemporary, with a grain of wisdom in its wit, says that "when the whites win a fight it is a victory, and when the Indians win it is a massacre!"
>
> *(Aberdeen Saturday Pioneer, 1891)*

Everywoman

When Baum wrote *The Wizard of Oz*, published in 1900, his children's book includes symbols of his contemporary world such as China and its Great Wall, parodied as "The Dainty China Country" in which porcelain people and animals are protected behind a wall and ruled by a "china princess." In a fine 1963 article in the *American Quarterly*, Henry M. Littlefield describes all the book's symbols, for example, Dorothy is "everyman"—in this case "everywoman" because Baum is a supporter of women's suffrage. The Scarecrow is the western farmer; the Tin Woodsman is the eastern factory worker; and the Cowardly Lion is none other than the pacifist politician William Jennings Bryan. And of course there are symbols of American Indians. The flying monkeys are a Darwinian reflection of where Baum and his fellow American citizens believed Indians and their cultures to be on the evolutionary scale. In the book, unlike the 1939 film, the flying monkeys talk. Littlefield points out that once the flying monkeys are freed from the grip of the Wicked Witch of the West (symbolizing the forces of nature) and "under the control of goodness and innocence," as personified by Dorothy, the monkeys are helpful and kind" (Littlefield 1963, 378). As Littlefield summarizes:

> Baum makes these Winged Monkeys into an Oz substitute for the plains Indians. Their leader says, "Once … we were a free people, living happily in the great forest, flying from tree to tree eating nuts and fruit, and doing just as we pleased without calling anybody master." This, he explains, "was many years ago, long before Oz [the United States and its capital, Washington, D.C.] came out of the clouds to rule over this land"
>
> (Littlefield 1963, 378)

How We Remember, Now

In 1896, anthropologist James Mooney published an official U.S.

government report, *The Ghost Dance Religion and the Sioux Outbreak of 1890*, issued by Mooney, who had made several field visits to Indians practicing the Ghost Dance and had interviewed Wovoka, the prophet of the religion. Mooney also was given access to the records of both the Indian Office and the War Department. He even had recordings made of the Ghost Dance songs with the cooperation of Emile Berliner and the Berliner Gramophone Company. Mooney then had these recordings transcribed by none other than the famous march composer John Philip Sousa and another musicologist, F.W.V. Gaisberg.

Virtually the entire range of American Indian studies are covered in this work. His work begins with a review of some of the lives of earlier Indian religious leaders such as the seventeenth century Pueblo leader Popé in what is now New Mexico. Mooney quotes Indian and non-Indian accounts of both the Ghost Dance and Wounded Knee. Mooney also included illustrations of a wide range of Ghost Dance objects and art that dramatically demonstrate American Indian esthetics that are rich in symbols. The volume includes some of the most important historic photographs and engravings of the ceremonies of the Ghost Dance and the horrors of the massacre at Wounded Knee (Mooney, 1896).

For First Nations, Wounded Knee remains a potent and sacred site. For example, in the 1960s, the Lakota artist Oscar Howe painted important canvases of the Ghost Dance and the oppression of industrialized America against Indian people. In 1973, the Lakota people and the American Indian Movement seized Wounded Knee as a protest of the murders permitted by the FBI and other American government officials at the Pine Ridge Reservation, South Dakota. The Canadian Metis artist Rick Rivet painted *Wounded Knee #2.* in 1991, reinterpreting an official U.S. photograph of the burial in a mass grave of distorted and frozen Lakota bodies. The bodies are reminiscent of the casts of those Romans killed at Pompeii, but this is no natural or inevitable tragedy.

Around the open grave, Rivet has replaced the American citizens of the original burial party with widely known figures of oppression including hooded members of the Ku Klux Klan and Nazi SS officers.

Robert Venables is senior lecturer at Cornell University, where his focus is on the Haudenosaunee (Six Nations) Confederacy. He has worked and testified on American Indian Nation cases in the courts of the U.S. and Canada.

References

Aberdeen Saturday Pioneer. 1890, Dec. 20. Microfilm in the Aberdeen Public Library, Aberdeen SD.

Aberdeen Saturday Pioneer. 1891, Jan. 3. Microfilm in the Aberdeen Public Library, Aberdeen SD.

Dixon, J. A. 1975. *The Vanishing Race.* New York: Bonanza.

Eastman, C. A. (Ohiyesa). 1916. *From Deep Woods to Civilization.* Reprinted Lincoln NE: University of Nebraska Press, 1977.

Flood, R. S. 1995. Lost Bird of Wounded Knee: Spirit of the Lakota. New York: Scribner.

Jackson, H. H. 1995. *Century of Dishonor: A Sketch of the United States Government's Dealings with Some of the Indian Tribes.* Norman OK: University of Oklahoma.

Jensen, R. E., R. E. Paul, and J. E. Carter. 1991. *Eyewitness at Wounded Knee.* Lincoln NE: University of Nebraska.

Littlefield, H. M. 1963. "The Wizard of Oz: Parable on Populism," *American Quarterly*, Vol. XV, No. 4 (Winter). In Cohen, H., ed. *The American Culture: Approaches to the Study of the United States.* Boston: Houghton Mifflin, 1968.

Miller, J. E., ed. 1959. "From Far Dakota's Cañons," *Leaves of Grass. Walt Whitman: Complete Poetry and Selected Prose.* Cambridge MA: Riverside/ Houghton Mifflin.

Mooney, J. 1896. *The Ghost-Dance Religion and Wounded Knee.* Reprinted New York: Dover, 1973.

Nast, T. 1878. "Patience Until the Indian Is Civilized—So To Speak," December 28. In Keller, M. *The art and politics of Thomas Nast.* New York: Oxford, 1968.

Nast, T. 1879. "Every Dog (No Distinction of Color Has) His Day," February 8. In Keller, M. 1968. *The Art and Politics of Thomas Nast.* New York: Oxford, 1968.

Neihardt, J. G. 1932. *Black Elk Speaks, Being the Life Story of a Holy Man of the Oglala Sioux.* Lincoln NE: University of Nebraska.

Prather, W. H. 1896. "The Indian Ghost Dance and War." In Mooney, J. 1973. *The Ghost-Dance Religion and Wounded Knee.* New York: Dover, 1973.

Riis, J. A. 1890. *How the Other Half Lives: Studies Among the Tenements of New York.* New York: Scribner's.

Weisberger, B. A. 1971. *The American Heritage of the American People.* New York: American Heritage.

U.S. Constitution: First Amendment
Religion and Expression
Congress shall make no law respecting an establishment of religion, or prohibiting the free exercise thereof; or abridging the freedom of speech, or of the press; or the right of the people peaceably to assemble, and to petition the Government for a redress of grievances.

The United States' Debt to American Indians

– By Robert J. Miller –

The United States owes a lot to the Indian Nations. Unquestionably, American Indians helped early European settlers to survive and succeed on this continent. And American Indian governments contributed mightily to the political thinking that led to the formation of the federal government that was created by our Founding Fathers.

The United States, however, also owes over 300,000 American Indians something else: for the mismanagement of their property over the past one hundred years the U.S. owes them around two hundred million dollars—making the mismanagement of Indian lands among the most expensive government scandals in American history.

One of the most surprising parts of this story is that few Americans know about it, and the media has been all but silent on it—even though this national debt has the potential to hit taxpayers in the pocket book.

It began in 1996 when the Native American Rights Fund filed a class action law suit, *Cobell v. Kempthorne*, against the United States for the mismanagement of tribal and individual Indian assets.

The case has already resulted in more than twelve federal court opinions, yet it has not even progressed beyond the discovery phase.

That's because the federal government and its attorneys have actively resisted this case every step of the way. Since 1999 two Cabinet Secretaries and the Assistant Secretary for Indian Affairs were held in contempt of court. These officials were fined more than 625,000 dollars for their violations.

Lamberth Removed

Federal District Court Judge Royce Lamberth was rewarded for his rulings last year when the D.C. Circuit Court of Appeals removed him from the case, alleging he had a growing bias in favor of the Indian plaintiffs.

In 1996, this case was discussed as being worth between two hundred billion and ten billion dollars in damages, which the U.S. either embezzled from Indians or had just "lost" through its incompetence. But today, the case is valued as possibly being worth up to two hundred billion dollars for the more than 300,000 plaintiffs. Attorney General Gonzalez has even opined that the tribal governments' claim for similar problems could result in this high of a verdict.

The case has arisen from the complicated history of federal Indian policies and because the United States became the trustee for the Indian Nations and individual Indian people.

Starting in 1887, with the passage of the *General Allotment Act*, the United States has been responsible for the oversight and management of most of the tribal and Indian land and assets in Indian country. As the trustee, the U.S. was responsible under trust law to reasonably lease and develop, and then to collect and pay the rents and profits from these assets to the Indian owners.

The allegation of the *Cobell* plaintiffs, and the widely accepted truth of the matter, is that the U.S. has failed miserably in exercising its fiduciary and trust responsibilities to carefully protect these assets and to collect the monies due and then to pay them to the Indian owners. Under the accepted law of trusts, the U.S. owes an accounting to the *Cobell* plaintiffs to identify all these funds and then to pay for any lost or uncollected funds due. The U.S. has actively resisted performing an accounting and seems to not want to find out what it owes these Indian people; people who are among the poorest of the poorest U.S. citizens.

The United States has claimed to the federal court that it would cost more than five hundred million dollars to perform an accounting for the past 120 years of its trusteeship over Indian assets. The U.S. appears to be fighting a rearguard action in court while hoping for some kind of legislative fix.

Many people would like to see the *Cobell* case disappear. Congress has twice already considered "midnight" riders to kill the case.

Senator John McCain and the Senate Committee on Indian Affairs have talked about proposing settlement amounts between seven-to-eight billion dollars and recent Senate and House bill have proposed these amounts.

Ending Trust

On March 1, 2007, the Bush administration responded to questions from the Senate Committee on Indian Affairs. The administration now proposes to settle all the trust mismanagement claims and to pay for all the needed Indian trust reform efforts with seven billion dollars. This is in spite of the acknowledged true price tag of the lost and mismanaged funds that could run into the hundreds of billions of dollars.

In their letter, Attorney General Alberto Gonzales and Interior Secretary Dirk Kempthorne told the Senate Committee that the administration was prepared to "invest" seven billion dollars to settle all trust mismanagement claims. At the same time the administration demands that the Congress extinguish the government's liability for all future trust claims. This last statement is the most egregious aspect of this sordid history.

The United States apparently wants to continue managing Indian assets but wants to prevent any future possible liability no matter how woefully it might manage and fail to protect these assets.

The proposal was immediately called a "bad faith offer" by the *Cobell* attorney. You might also think this was a bad faith settlement if it were your assets that the U.S. controlled but wanted to avoid any responsibility for doing so in a careful and responsible manner.

Senator Byron Dorgan (D-ND.), the chairman of the Senate Committee Indian Affairs, said: "This is the first time that the federal government has acknowledged a multi-billion dollar liability for the mismanagement of the Indian trust funds over the past century and more. That is a significant admission."

A more significant admission would be for the United States to live up to the debt it owes these Indian people and to account for and pay them the money that is legally theirs but which has been mismanaged and withheld from them for the past one hundred years.

Robert J. Miller *is a law professor at Lewis & Clark College in Portland, Oregon, the chief justice of the Grand Ronde Tribe, and an enrolled citizen of the Eastern Shawnee Tribe of Oklahoma. He is also the author of the new book* "Native America, Discovered and Conquered: Thomas Jefferson, Lewis & Clark, and Manifest Destiny."

The Aliens Amongst Us, or The People of Sacred Corn

– By Roberto Rodriguez and Patrisia Gonzales –

W
e were being interviewed about our "San Ce Tojuan" documentary on Indigenous memory and the relatedness of all the peoples of the continent, when the phone started ringing off the hook. We had asked listeners of a Spanish-language radio station to call in and speak in their Native tongues. The telephone lines in Madison, WI, smoked with Zapotec, Otomie, Nahuatl, Maya and Mixteco speakers. This was not news to us because we know that Otomie elders come north of the border to perform naming ceremonies and bless placentas. Mixteco women organize collectives in the San Joaquin Valley while Nahua women with their rebozos, or traditional shawls, participate in parenting forums for "Latino" families in the snowy white community of Madison.

Indian Country is changing all over the hemisphere as Indigenous people refuse to become "the disappeared," especially at a time when Evo Morales of Bolivia is not simply Bolivia's president, but arguably the president of Indigenous America.

Since the 1960s, much of the migration from Mexico has been from largely rural populations in states with high Indigenous populations. They are the ones who still place their hands in the earth in both Mexico and the United States. With the wars in Central America of the 1970s and 1980s came the Mayas. Also, numerous Indigenous peoples of the southern cone, such as the Quechua, are settling in places such as New York. And when Indigenous delegates arrive to the United Nations, often hailing from populations in Guatemala, Peru, Ecuador and Bolivia, they connect with the networks of the Indigenous diaspora who assert the right to act communally in the United States.

Uncomfortable Truth

It is often said that this nation was founded upon slavery. While accurate, it would be more accurate to say that it was founded upon, genocide and land theft... and slavery. This genocide was not strictly physical, but also included a genocide of truth, a genocide of memory and a genocide of narrative. This genocide created the first *desaparecidos* or "the disappeared," by wrenching our ancestors and knowledge(s) from their descendants—the original peoples of Turtle Island or Pacha Mama. In fact, first to disappear was Pacha Mama. In its place: the Americas. And then the people became Indians, and shortly thereafter, mestizos—peoples purportedly not Indigenous and detached from Pacha Mama.

For many U.S. citizens, all this constitutes uncomfortable truths... not so much because of this ignoble past, but because those genocidal legacies live with us to this day, particularly in terms of how Indigenous peoples are viewed and treated in the United States and throughout this continent. This is most especially true in terms of how this nation views and treats Mexicans and Central Americans, and sometimes South Americans also. These peoples—regardless of legal status—are generally viewed and treated as unwelcome, suspect, illegitimate and nowadays, illegal. And chillingly, these attitudes are beginning to be codified into draconian anti-immigrant laws and ordinances in towns and cities both near and far from the U.S.-Mexico border. Many of these laws pertain to denial of housing and social services, as well as language and cultural enforcement. Not coincidentally, these laws and ordinances do not target Canadians, Europeans or Russian immigrants. Similarly, all this also is being punctuated with legislation that calls for the erection of hundreds of miles of militarized fences and walls along the U.S.-Mexico-border—along with aggressive hunter battalions (the U.S. Customs and Border Patrol) charged specifically with chasing down red-brown peoples anywhere in the country in a modern-day policy of Indian Removal.

As noted, society's insistence upon continuing to divide up people into legal and illegal categories isn't simply a matter of how peoples are

Shoot the Indian © 2005 Frank Salcido

perceived; it also manifests in dividing people up into human beings with full human rights, and those with fewer rights. Not surprisingly, those in the suspect and illegal categories are primarily red-brown peoples, peoples that society has misnamed Hispanics. This term, which is imposed upon peoples who already rejected en masse two hundred years ago the colonization of the Americas by Spain, includes both Indigenous, and what Mexican scholar Guillermo Bonfil Batalla terms, "de-Indigenized Indians" or mestizos (*Mexico Profundo*, 1996). As he notes, an imaginary Mexico has been created by taking away what is "Indian." Yet that which is Indian in Mexico is so pervasive that what remains is still Indian. All of these peoples, Mexican scholar Enrique Florescano, asserts, also constitute part of the living culture of Mesoamerica—the thousands-of-years-old maize-based culture from Mexico and Central America (*Memoria Indigena* 1999). And many of these peoples, rather than sit back and wait to be harassed, are nowadays asserting their ancestral rights to live here as full human beings. The year 2006 saw the massive mobilization of millions of Mexicans and Central and South Americans and their allies in protest of anti-immigrant measures. Many Indigenous peoples marched not as immigrants but as the original peoples of this continent. Beyond protesting, many are now openly asserting the right to take their/our rightful place in this society, many are also asserting the right to partake in thousands-of-years old traditions, customs and rituals.

The Maize

Whereas U.S. society sees an invasion of brown hordes, we see families. Whereas society sees aliens, we see people doing what they've been doing for thousands of years—that is, migrating. Whereas this society clings to colonizing and fictionalized narratives (narratives that begin in 1492), our peoples have much older histories and narratives. These include thousands-of years-old maize narratives that are shared by many peoples of this continent (some can even be seen in the two-thousand-year-plus San Bartolo murals in Guatemala that depict the ancient Mayan *Popul Vuh* —the ancient story of Maize and creation).

Maize, in effect, is who we are—people of corn—a people who have a documented history on this continent for many thousands of years. We are defined by our own histories and narratives—as found in oral traditions and in the many ancient Mexican/Central American

Indigenous codices, and not by the actions of Columbus or any other conquistador. If anything, these traditions are kept alive by stories, songs, dances, rituals, ceremonies, customs and traditions… and by our daily sustenance.

Yet, while we have these stories, in a nation that views itself through a black-white binary, it is seemingly difficult to find a place for Indigenous peoples in this society—except in the realm of either denial or long-ago-history best forgotten. Seemingly even more difficult is finding a place for the red-brown peoples from south that have been increasingly migrating into the United States, so much so, that many so-called nativists warn of an ongoing silent invasion. The truth is, red-brown peoples have been migrating from the south since they brought maize from Southern Mexico into what is today the United States some 5,000 years ago… and again 2,000 years ago when the Hohokam also brought corn and corn culture northward into what is today the U.S. Southwest, and truthfully, Indigenous peoples have been migrating in all directions since time immemorial (Jack Forbes, Aztecas del Norte, 1973).

We suggest that the fear of the "browning of the nation" is actually a fear of the re-Indigenization or the Indigenization of the entire continent. In the mindset of many of these xenophobes, the number of brown people is supposed to be decreasing, not increasing. That's what Providence and Manifest Destiny were supposed to be all about: the civilization and de-indigenization of the continent. In plain-speak, that means the extermination of Indigenous peoples.

Beyond mischaracterizing these migrations as invasions, this view is dependant upon viewing these peoples as illegitimate… which is nothing new. Instead, it is an extension of the original European project of declaring the continent void of humanity and empty of human beings, by which was meant Christians. Thus, to view Mexicans and Central Americans in this country as illegitimate and nowadays illegal is little different than when the first Europeans questioned the humanity of Indigenous peoples on this continent. It is an extension of their narrative.

Ethnocide

To do this required that genocide of truth, memory and narrative. This included the assertion that Indigenous peoples were both outside of God and history. They were purportedly not entitled to live, possess lands or have their own history and worldview. They were, however, entitled to live if they renounced everything about themselves, and swore loyalty and gave freely of their labor to the King of Spain and the Church. These delusional beliefs, along with European greed and Indigenous resistance is what triggered the greatest genocides in the history of humanity (aided by foreign diseases). What followed is an ethnocide that continues; to this day, brown people are supposed to view themselves as either descending from peoples who were demonic, or who had no history prior to 1492. That's why for many self-identified nativists, indigenous Mexicans and Central Americans as illegal aliens computes. Mexicans/Central Americans as full human beings… does not.

That's why part of this societal view includes never viewing these brown peoples—our relatives, as Indigenous. At best, they are assigned the category of mongrels—peoples not worthy of being afforded the dignity of being either fully human nor being worthy of being afforded full human rights. Many people forget that the oppressive Spanish caste system imposed during the three hundred-year colonial era was not necessarily a system of racial categorization. Instead, it was a system that was part and parcel to colonialism, which on this continent ensured the dehumanization of non-Europeans. The caste system itself was designed to determine which human beings had full rights (Europeans)… and who merited partial rights or no rights at all. This is where notions of mongrelization—with accompanying fancy names and dozens of categories—became systematized. The term mestizo derives from this very system. It was not a racial descriptor, but a category that said: You are not a full human being, and certainly, you are not entitled to the same rights afforded to full human beings (read European Christians).

Humanity Denied

As Sharon Venne has pointed out in *Our Elders Know Our Rights* (1998), the colonial debate about whether Indigenous peoples were truly human was actually not about whether they were biologically human, but about whether they were entitled to full human rights. In this sense, this too was the objective of the Spanish caste system.

Can it not be said that the same logic is in place today? Regardless of their stated purposes, codified racial/ethnic categories on this continent are a reminder that some human beings are afforded more rights than others… or that some people are considered more human than other. Is this not what the rejection of red-brown peoples in this society tells us? The maintenance of these modern racial categorical schemes tells us that we continue to live in a society not of full human beings, but a society increasingly divided into full human beings and peoples considered less than human. Into this milieu is the rabid xenophobia that threatens to further divide this country into a society of legal and illegal human beings. The irony of course is that it is Indigenous peoples from this continent—who have never been to Europe—that are being remanded into these illegal categories.

A further irony is that the arguments continue in some quarters—even in Indian country—as to whether Mexicans/Central Americans are actually Indigenous. Some assert that they are not; that they in fact are mestizos or half-breeds… not Indigenous. This is the absurdity of what Western society has bequeathed us; a ferocious debate over notions of legality and illegality and over questions of Indigenous authenticity. Are Mexicans/Central Americans half-Indigenous? One quarter? Blood quantum—part of the U.S. colonial project—has nowadays been injected into this debate… Don't they speak a colonial language (Spanish… as if English were not also a colonial language)? Rather than asserting the full humanity of these peoples, this society has us questioning their/our breed… and their/our rightful place in this society. All of these categories and all of these systems of identification have one thing in common; they are arguably part of centuries-old de-Indigenization or Indian extermination projects. Of course, most of the land has already been stolen (occupied America)… and in effect, so too the people (occupied minds). To complete this project requires that genocide of narrative. But regardless of how hard society tries, the thousands-of-years-old maize narratives cannot be completely erased because they are everywhere… mostly hidden in plain sight.

Kernels of Wisdom

We remember a time when a Nahuatl elder addressed some visiting Mexican American teachers at Nahuatl University in Morelos, Mexico. She told them: "Most of you have lost your original [Indigenous] language, your ways and your traditions… but don't for one second doubt that you are indigenous. But if you ever do, eat a tortilla."

This was a simple reminder that yes, we've been subjected to centuries of colonialism, but as peoples, we survive. And equally important, our stories survive… stories revolving around our thousands-of-years-old maize cultures. Perhaps we cannot claim to have come out of colonialism unscathed… (most of us are displaced peoples), but we in fact are part of maize culture. After all, what is Mexican/Central American culture without maize… without the tortilla? Funny thing about colonialism… the colonialists took the gold, the silver and the land, but they could not destroy the sacred sustenance of the people… Centeotzintli or sacred maize. Centeotzintli is more than what we eat or who we are. It is also where we come from. As scientists say: We are what we eat… and in that sense, what we eat is maize, beans and squash… and chile… plus nopal (cactus), etc. These are foods that not only have not been eliminated, but are increasing in importance, primarily because they are healthy and are the antidote to heart disease, obesity and diabetes, etc.

Taino writer José Barreiro once told us that the mestizo is either one less Indian or one more Indian waiting to reemerge. In a sense, that is the metaphor of all the red-brown peoples streaming across the artificially imposed U.S.-Mexico border. For us, to be Indigenous is a synonym for being a human being. And yet, perhaps we don't need to enter into rhetorical debates over whether Mexicans/Central Americans are in fact Indigenous. What we assert is that Mexicans/Central Americans are part of an ancient and living maize culture… a culture that is affirmed virtually every time we eat a meal. And as a friend and Choctaw law student Alicia Seyler once told us, "Isn't that the definition of Indigenous?"

Can Mexicans/Central Americans derive power (political or otherwise) simply from asserting thousands-of-years-old ties and affiliation to maize culture? Other elders have told us that people cease being peoples when they no longer have stories. So in that sense, it begins with our stories… with our narratives. We belong because we have always belonged. That's the first step of power, belonging. But that assumes that that's what we want, power. Perhaps we simply want to take on the role of our relatives, not as masters, but as caretakers of our Mother.

Roberto Rodriguez and *Patrisia Gonzales* *write the Column of the Americas and are both finishing their PhDs in Communications at the University of Wisconsin at Madison. They are syndicated columnists and longtime journalists.*

Media Do's and Don'ts

– By Celilo Village Elders with Carol Craig –

F irst the U.S. Army Corps of Engineers moved Celilo village from the riverbanks of the Columbia River and the site of their millenia-old trade and fishing center. They chipped the petroglyphs from the cliffsides doomed to be underwater and carted them away. They bombed the black basalt center out of the falls to carve a commercial shipping lane—picture a beautiful woman with her teeth knock out. And at 10 a.m. March 10, 1957 the inch-thick reinforced steel gates of the Dalles Dam in Central Oregon crashed shut, forcing a ferocious backflow of the ancient river that in four and one-half hours—while women from the village with children in hand cried—flooded everything in its way.

* * * *

In January 2007 the elders of the village, who were children when Celilo Falls was destroyed, began meeting to discuss how to cope with the public interest in the fifty-year anniversary. Working with staff from the Columbia Intertribal Fish Commission and Carol Craig, public information officer from the Yakama Nation, the Celilo elders identified a list of expectations for behavior by reporters and photographers who covered the anniversary. Craig and other volunteers asked journalists covering the commemoration events to read and sign this list.

On March 10, 2007 several journalists said they appreciated having this direction from our elders.

–Kara Briggs, Editor

DO

- Ask for permission when taking photos of individuals. Crowds are okay.
- Take names of people in pictures you have taken including tribal affiliation.
- Join the people when they are dining.
- Ask questions about the event.
- Request photos of Celilo Chief Olsen Meanus and he will receive a copy of each photo taken.
- Let the people know where you are from, TV station, newspaper, magazine, other.
- Inside longhouse when Washat services are not taking place ask permission to take pictures.
- If/when in the kitchen area ask who is in charge and if okay to take pictures.

DON'T

- Assume it is all right to take a person's picture without their permission.
- Take any pictures of drummers and singers during Washat Service inside longhouse.
- Crowd in front of elders and others to take photos without their permission.
- Any photos taken will not be for resale.
- Walk on the dirt floor inside the longhouse.
- Take pictures of anyone wearing tags requesting no pictures be taken of them.
- Forget to thank people you interview or take pictures of.
- Take pictures of powwow and stick game participants without permission.

I _____ *(print name)* have read the above list about taking photographs or interviewing tribal people in attendance during the Celilo Memorial March 10–11, 2007 and will comply with the agreement.

Date _____, Signed _____

Nation Building:
The Fight for Native Women's Human Rights

– By Kara Briggs –

For a moment in 2006, a moment as brief as a flash of lightening, Cecilia Fire Thunder captured the usually single-minded attention of those on either side of the abortion debate. Fire Thunder is a plain-spoken nurse who built a national reputation in the 1990s teaching survivors of sexual abuse that sex can be good. Her stand was less an unsubtle play for attention than a misstep in candor—a step that cost her the presidency of the Oglala Lakota Nation.

I traveled to South Dakota in early June of that year ostensibly looking for Fire Thunder in the midst of the ferocious campaign to ban abortion in absolutely every case. The ban, which would have made it a crime for doctors to perform an abortion with no exceptions for rape or incest, had been passed by the state legislature earlier in the year in an effort to establish a national test case that could overthrow *Roe v. Wade*. With the landmark 1973 U.S. Supreme Court ruling out of the way—South Dakota strategists theorized, states would be free to set their own abortion laws—laws which in the coastal blue states would likely stay much as they are today, laws that in the red interior states would probably send abortion rights the way of the dinosaur.

What I found on the back roads between Yankton, Rosebud and Pine Ridge, underneath the handmade pro-ban signs showing blond-haired Gerber babies, was a fabric of Native women taking care of women, taking care of Native girls, taking care of each other. It's an epic story untold in media, whether mainstream or Indian. It's untold,

I think, because women are not part of mainstream society's limited perception about who the mythic Indian is.

The Brave Heart Society

The role of women in tribal cultures, whether historic or contemporary, is perhaps the most critical misunderstanding of tribal values by mainstream society. Mainstream American society's colonial influence through schooling and through mass media is so profound that even many Native peoples are disconnected from the profound role that women played and still play in Native cultures. This results in "internalized oppression," say many women leaders, which makes itself evident in the rampant domestic violence, sexual violence and family violence among tribal America.

White men contribute to the familial violence against Native women so dramatically that they skew national interracial violence statistics, which show that Natives suffer interracial violence at a higher rate than all other races. That such violence, from white or Native perpetrators, is more likely to happen in the bedroom than on the street, doesn't show up in the public record. Nor does the leading role that Native women—some of whom may have survived such abuse—are playing in rebuilding the fabric of Native America.

Yet in a high school gymnasium, smelling of ammonia from its end-of-the-school-year cleaning, I witnessed as clear an example of nation building as I've seen reported on any of the twenty-four hour news networks in years.

Gathered in that gym because the house across the dusty Lake Andes, S.D., street was too small to hold all the women, Faith Spotted Eagle told about the re-emergence of the Brave Heart Society.

Historically, this society went onto battle fields to recover the tribe's dead and bring them home again. In the last decade, a group of female leaders among the Yankton Sioux decided that a work was needed to reclaim girls for the tribe, girls who'd drifted too young into unhealthy sexual relationships fueled by alcohol and drugs, who'd borne children or who'd sought abortions, who were drifting farther and faster downstream than generations that had come before them.

The South Dakota women began searching for the key to helping these girls. Their quest took them to the archives, where they particularly sought the writings of Ella Cara Deloria, a Yankton ethnologist born in 1889. Deloria wanted her writings to reflect a time before her birth when Nakota culture existed as it had for millennia without the intrusion of white culture. Her novel *Waterlily,* portrays the daily life of a woman, whose marriage to a jealous, abusive man collapses while she is pregnant with their child. Yet *Waterlily,* the title character, finds her way in the kinship systems, which elsewhere Deloria explained, defined as the heart of Nakota life.

In Deloria's writing, the grandmothers found what they wanted to offer to the young women of their tribe. It was the kind of kinship relationships that had guided their nation since before the oldest memory, Madonna Archambeau remembered.

"We have to stake ourselves down," said Archambeau, a former chairwoman of the Yankton Sioux. "If we don't, we'll just be brown people fighting for equality."

But, how? Spotted Eagle, a post-traumatic-distress-order counselor, described taking twenty young mothers to the Black Hills for the society's first camp.

"We sat up there like you would in school, and we kind of chastised them," Spotted Eagle said. "But when you place yourself in these sacred places, things will start to come back."

One of the young mothers began to shake under a power outside herself, Spotted Eagle recalled. That's when ceremony began. It was unplanned by organizers, yet it was in the deepest tradition of their people. It was the ceremony that could heal unseen wounds. When the women came home, they asked the still-older grandmothers for a name for this group. The elder women named it the Brave Heart Society.

"Symbolically, we are bringing girls back from emotional death," Spotted Eagle said.

The Backbones

This is critically important, Archambeau told the group gathered in the gym, because these girls will grow into the backbones of their nations.

"When it comes to making something happen," Archambeau said, "it's the women."

Standing with her teenaged granddaughter by her side, Archambeau went on to quote the late Snohomish leader Janet McCloud, "We may no longer be strong nations of people. We know that. Look around you, what we do have are strong families and strong extended families." Families, Archambeau said, are centered around women.

Yet this insight about the significance of Native women, which is internationally true across Native America, is lost in media coverage and academic research which all but overlooks Native women leaders. In the last twenty-five years the number women elected leaders of tribes has doubled. By 2007 women led more than one-quarter of tribal councils, according to the National Congress of the American Indian. Three years ago a new organization called Women Empowering Women for Indian Nations was organized by some of these women elected leaders to mentor and support others. For many years women have held key staff positions in most of the 562 federally recognized tribal governments, and in leadership roles in the vast network of Native American non-profits.

Monica Davey of the *New York Times* notes some of these facts in a February 8, 2006, article titled "As Tribal Leaders, Women Still Fight Old Views." As Davey acknowledged, old perceptions die hard.

An Earlier Status Quo

A century ago white male researchers bypassed women to speak to the men, said Ann McCormack, coordinator of cultural resources for the Nez Perce in Idaho. These researchers set forth America's base understanding of tribes, which is reflected today in our text books, in our media portrayals and in our popular literature. Combine this misperception with the tendency of both tribal and white news organizations to only quote elected tribal leaders, who are still majority male, and then only about whatever developments involve enough money or real estate to be deemed newsworthy.

Leadership roles come naturally for many tribal women, who before white contact often held powerful positions in their nations, including suffrage and political leadership, property and business ownership. Centuries of bombardment with male-oriented European values in boarding schools, in Christian churches and in the U.S. government, which chose to work exclusively with tribal men.

Still in the 1970s when feminism spread like wild fire across white America, many Native women expressed ambivalence. We were only going back to what had been the status quo many generations ago, several Native women leaders told me in the last year. White women were striving for an equality that they'd never had before.

Its from the ancient tradition of women's leadership in the Americas that contemporary women come to the real work of nation building in Native America.

Societal Transformation

Nation building was defined at the outset of the Iraq War by the Carnegie Endowment for International Peace as being for the purpose of changing or propping up regimes, involving deployment of troops and engaging in a nation's political structures. The same year Rand Corporation, a U.S. think tank, offered a broader definition, which I cite here, of bringing about fundamental societal transformations. This is what I contend Native women in tribal and in urban Indian communities are doing as they reach out to help other women, typically heads of households with dependant children and elders.

This work is most critical in South Dakota, a place where in 1999 the U.S. Commission on Civil Rights found a state of racial polarization: "Despair is not too strong a word to characterize the emotional feelings of many Native Americans who believe they live in a hostile environment." In the spring and summer of 2006, the mood among tribal women working on reproductive health issues in South Dakota was definitely one of being under siege.

Yet they defined sexual violence and substance abuse as critical issues to the national security of tribal nations. Here I am defining failures of national security as the long-term lack of law enforcement from inside or outside tribal nations on certain felony cases, which build on familiar long-standing societal problems.

Charon Asetoyer, the Comanche director of the Native Women's Health Education Resource Center in Lake Andes, S.D., sees this daily in the triple threat of violence, poverty and teen pregnancy.

"It's because of famine that we have a food pantry, and we move twenty to thirty tons of food a year," Asetoyer said. "When we see famine, we think lower Saharan Africa. But having three kids and no food in your refrigerator, that's famine."

A Big If

The choice to bear children may be limited already in Native

America where rates of reported rape are 3.5% higher than among other American races. Add to that the complications in the largely rural South Dakota in getting access to rape kits, to emergency contraceptives and to law enforcement follow up. On reservations, the FBI is charged with investigating felonies such as rape or incest. But that's only if the case is reported as rape, a decision of the Indian Health Service, the federal agency that is the primary local health care provider for reservations.

"That's a big if," Asetoyer said. "Once a woman has been raped, the trauma she is experiencing is extremely high. The last thing she wants is to be put in a car and travel one hundred miles (to Sioux Falls) for another examination. The re-traumatization that she feels is traumatizing in itself. This is one of the leading health problems in Indian Country."

It's into this context that Cecilia Fire Thunder uttered her determination to open a reproductive health clinic on her allotment in the Northeast corner of the Pine Ridge reservation in March 2006. She uttered it to Native columnist Tim Giago. When it appeared in print, the reproductive health clinic had turned into an abortion clinic. Fire Thunder, a nurse who once worked in an abortion clinic in California, didn't back away from the idea. Soon, via the Internet, the first elected chairwoman of the Oglala Sioux was poster woman or kicking post of the abortion wars, depending on which side you're on.

Throughout the spring of 2006 I ran into Native women, old enough to have grown daughters and granddaughters, talking admiringly about Fire Thunder's outspoken stand. At one tribal elders' lunch in Western Washington, several women in discussing the situation in Pine Ridge said they wouldn't want to return to the days of coat-hanger abortions.

Women's Conversations

By the time I reached Pine Ridge, traveling by car across the back roads from Yankton through Rosebud in the company of Mohawk midwife Katsi Cook and Mohawk Bear Clan Mother Louise McDonald, I heard the familiar debate again, though this time it was stated in an unfamiliar style—one that was sincere and polite. Katsi (pronounced Gud-je), midwife and prominent advocate for reproductive health in Indian Country, declared the right to an abortion a matter of sexual justice for women. Historically, she said tribal women had access to this kind of care by women who held the knowledge of such matters. Now women need to be afforded the choice, Katsi said, speaking as much as a midwife as a tribal woman with grown children.

"You cannot be a woman-centered culture and not offer abortion," Katsi Cook said.

Louise responded with her quiet discomfort. Like people of many faiths, she, a woman who conducts ancient ceremonies for women, didn't know whether she could stretch her deeply held beliefs to endorse abortion as a choice.

Louise is like women on many reservations. She focuses her work on youth, particularly on giving youth a foundation that she hopes will help them avoid the pitfalls of early sexual activity and substance abuse. Louise has helped develop on the Akwesasne reservation puberty rites, which extend for several years of tutelage in tribal culture.

"I didn't want my child's idea of coming of age to be graduating from high school, getting a driver's license, getting liquored up or getting laid," she said.

Arriving in Pine Ridge, the Mohawk women headed for sun dance grounds in the Black Hills while I hung around the reservation conducting interviews and hoping to make contact with Fire Thunder before my looming deadline (my plane ticket home). Finally, I raised the president on my cell from the town of Pine Ridge, but reception was poor. I went to a gas station, and called her home at Martin, S.D., from a pay phone.

Fire Thunder

I asked for an in-person interview. Fire Thunder blurted out, "Indian women are so out of touch with their vaginas."

What might seem from someone else to be an off-hand comment was from Fire Thunder—already in early June embattled, on suspension and facing second of three impeachment hearing—a shorthanded assessment of one of Indian Country's deepest, darkest secrets. For Fire Thunder, the rampant sexual abuse of Indian children and women should be at the top of every tribal council agenda in country. I agree. But Fire Thunder's political skill was honed in family, in hospitals and in conferences where she was a popular speaker. That's a different training ground than the close-to-the-ground democracies of tribal

America. She couldn't carry the message and ultimately hold onto the presidency against the pressures from her political opponents.

Meeting me at the First Peoples Fund in Rapid City a week before her impeachment hearing, she explained, "I got really angry about a bunch of white guys making decisions about my body."

One Woman-Centered Culture

The white guys in this case were the South Dakota Legislature and Governor Mike Rounds. As men, Fire Thunder explained, they would not be allowed under the traditional divisions of labor in Lakota culture to speak about women's health issues, let alone to tell women what to do. Quickly her tone turned to mocking—as might be heard among women elders—over men who would dabble in such obvious women's business.

Her tone didn't come from the state-wide political movement against the ban. It grew from her childhood growing up on the rural reservation with seven sisters and a mother and father who loved them.

Recalling the care that her father, a singer of Indian songs, gave her, tears ran down Fire Thunder's cheeks. Bringing his girls home in winter, she remembers him leaving them in the warm car while he went into the cold house to warm up their blankets by the fire. Then he returned and carried his daughters, one-by-one to their beds and tucked them in the warmth.

"Even in 1987 when I was forty-seven or forty-eight years old, my dad would call us 'baby' and 'my pretty little girls'," she said. "The benefits of this love is immeasurable. All my sisters are pretty successful because we all grew up with this sense that we could do anything."

She was an adult before she realized that her father and mother had carefully planned their births so they fell two years apart, out of concern for the health of mother and children.

Woman to Woman

As a nurse in California and a divorced mother of sons, Fire Thunder saw a different view of life. When she was assigned to work one day a week in an abortion clinic, her supervisor asked her to be a friend to her patients, to walk them through, to speak to them woman to woman. Sometime in these years she read an article about an abortion clinic bombing. She began to imagine a such a clinic on a reservation, where the tribal nation could control who came on the reservation and could presumably keep such violence out.

In the early 1990s, she created a sexual awareness workshop for Native women, a workshop that spoke plainly about the difference between healthy sexuality and abuse. The workshops ran for a decade, and Fire Thunder got a view on the profound lack of awareness about abusive behaviors across Indian America.

"It was a learning journey," she said. "I spent a lot of time in Canada. Canadian Native nations really owned this stuff long before we have. It wasn't only the abuse in their residential schools, but also the abuse in their communities. In Canada they prepared me to talk about this at home."

This epidemic abuse has long legs, stretching from generation to generation since the early days of government-enforced attendance at boarding schools. Eighty-five percent of the Indian women in treatment for drug and alcohol abuse, Fire Thunder said, will at some point in the treatment cycle disclose being sexually abused.

A Fair Shake

Now, I've read just about every article published about Fire Thunder. But I've never read the kind of material I am writing here. I don't think that I was the only reporter who was hearing some of this information. I do think that, with the exception of a couple of Native reporters and *Indian Country Today's* David Melmer, I was the only one who could give this context, who could remember reading fliers for her workshop, who could give a whole afternoon to an interview. On the day I met Fire Thunder, she was excited about a *Rapid City Journal* article that she felt gave her a fair shake. Promising that Fire Thunder would speak despite a tribal council attempt to stop her, the article spent most of its paragraphs quoting other people about Fire Thunder speaking and ended with a not-particularly interesting quote from her.

I think by "fair," Fire Thunder meant that the article wasn't an overt attack on her.

Fire Thunder was impeached on June 29, though reinstated a few weeks later when an Oglala Sioux Tribal Court judge found that the council in its haste to get rid of her had violated her freedom of speech under both the *Indian Civil Rights Act* and the Oglala Sioux Tribe's Constitution. She was impeached again in late July, and lost a re-election bid.

I mentioned problematic coverage of Fire Thunder, notably in the online magazine *Salon*, during an ethics discussion at the Journalism and Women's Symposium. A white women from a women's journalism foundation dismissed my criticism of *Salon*, saying that Fire Thunder had already made so many mistakes. This woman then turned away from me and also the young black journalist sitting next to me.

Time for Change

White feminists were quick to canonize Fire Thunder in 2006—sprinkling the tribal office in Pine Ridge with several hundred personal checks for five and ten dollars each to support her work on the basis of on the personal blog report that *Salon* reprinted unconfirmed. These feminists were equally quick to drop her. Like a ham-handed CIA interference in a foreign government's operations, white feminists' patronizing donations unknowingly contributed to the disarray around this issue in the Oglala Sioux national government. They participated in Fire Thunder's political downfall. Eventually, the Oglala Nation returned their checks.

Yet speaking as a Native journalist, the pursuit of Fire Thunder's story gave me insight into the women across tribal America who are standing up against the violence and poverty that continues to threaten the very future of tribal nations. The danger of this threat is most clear in the context of our own rhetoric about our concern for the seventh generation and about the children being are our future.

As Fire Thunder told me, "The abortion issue is the key that opened the padlock to the sexual deviancy on the reservation."

Kara Briggs is associate director of the American Indian Policy and Media Initiative. She worked eighteen years in daily newspapers, most recently the Oregonian *in Portland, Oregon.*

Introduction to Three Pieces About the Haudenosaunee and New York State

It's been two centuries since the Six Nations Iroquois, known among themselves as Haudenosaunee, known as the people of the longhouse, influenced American democracy. Now their ancestral lands in New York State and Canada are again centers for anti-Indian activity.

Lawn signs in quiet Central New York towns read "No Sovereign Lands," as if wishful but uninformed rhetoric could turn back 10,000 years of history and four hundred years of treaty making with colonizing forces by the Seneca, Cayuga, Onondaga, Oneida, Mohawk and Tuscarora Nations.

Yet the next three chapters will examine how the mainstream news media, anti-Indian hate groups and the U.S. Supreme Court have united in recent years to erode the sovereignty of the Six Nations. The first report, "Twin Polls Show Media and Government Out of Step with the Public," deals with a content analysis of newspapers in Upstate New York and how they reported on the New York Legislatures efforts to tax goods purchased on reservations. It focuses on a study by the American Indian Policy and Media Initiative with communication students at Buffalo State College and on another study by Zogby International.

The second chapter, "Shaping Public Opinion: Slanted Coverage in Central New York," uses a content analysis by the author to analyze how two newspapers covered the lead up to the 2005 U.S. Supreme Court's rejection of the Oneida Nation's right to buy back ancestral land in *City of Sherrill v. Oneida Nation* in New York.

Content surveys are important for observing how the media set agendas by indicating through language, sourcing, and story order what readers should think. They are also important for observing that the media also select a perspective or a frame for reporting on each issue.

The third chapter, "The Enlightened Racist and the Anti-Gaming Movement," examines the role of particular hate groups in encouraging New York and Ontario to challenge the sovereignty of the Haudenosaunee nations.

José Barreiro editorialized in a 2005 edition of *Indian Country Today* about the influence of these anti-Indian forces on the U.S. Supreme Court in the *Sherrill* case, stating that "the court guided itself, in large measure by the cacophony of voices that raised the anti-Indian volume, in newspapers and state discourse." The court followed the Oneida decision quickly with what Barreiro called "a near-genocidal blow" in rejecting the Cayuga land claim. The Cayuga alone among the Iroquois don't have land within their ancestral territory.

From an outsider's perspective, the contrast between the profound leadership and history of the Six Nations and the modern backlash they are enduring is striking.

The Haudenosaunee provided a model for the U.S., not only of how to run a union of states, but also since the mid-1900s in reasserting sovereignty after the abrogation of every treaty, leading tribal nations into international circles and informing Native America through the ground-breaking publication, *Akwesasne Notes*.

In 1992 at the historic gathering of one hundred Native leaders at "Our Visions: The Next 500 Years" in Taos, New Mexico, Oren Lyons, Faithkeeper of the Onondaga Nation, said, "Nobody gives you sovereignty. You take sovereignty." That sentiment has informed the Haudenosaunee for centuries, and runs today through the veins of the people.

Still, *Indian Country Today* editor Randi Rourke, Mohawk, watches the backlash. She wonders if it isn't all misdirected frustration that would be more appropriately aimed at local governments and state legislatures. The backlash is dangerous, she said, and is fueling an ideological revision in the proud history of the Haudenosaunee's lessons to a young nation.

"We existed as nations on this land for centuries before it became known as 'America,' Rourke said. "Our collective strength, from living in harmony with nature and one another, was symbolized by a bundle of arrows bound together. Lately, we are seeing more threats to these ideas, a refusal to acknowledge our role in American history and even now, in the present. It's a battle, but there are many warriors among us."

–Kara Briggs, Editor

Two Polls Show Media and Government Out of Step with the Public

– By Ronald D. Smith –

I t makes for an interesting and unusual image—public opinion marching down the path of social progress; government and the news media on the other side, out of step with the people who make up the media-using citizenry.

The specifics of this report deal with taxation proposals in New York State, but close your eyes and you'll see the obvious parallels throughout the country in dozens of situations in which states tell Indian tribes and nations what they should or should not do, or what the state would like to do to them. Because fundamentally, this report deals with the issue of Indian sovereignty. It focuses on two polls released within last year that documented the high level of public opinion for so-called Indian issues—one by college students, the other by a professional polling organization.

Student Research: The Public Gets It; Media, Not So Much

Students at Buffalo State College conducted a four-part research project during Spring 2005. Their project had two goals: to identify and understand public opinion toward Indian issues, and to correlate this with how the mainstream news media report about those issues.

The study was conducted by students in the college's Communication Department as part of a senior-level course, Applied Communication

Research, conducted by three professors: Dr. Rik Whitaker, Dr. Marian Deutschman, and Professor Ronald D. Smith. The latter is project director for the school's American Indian Policy and Media Initiative.

The students began with a literature review concerning various Indian issues—sovereignty, treaty rights, and New York State's then-current public policy brawl over taxation of goods sold on Native lands.

The twenty-six-student class then conducted a series of focus groups that yielded a generally positive profile of a citizenry that can best be described as friendly and open toward Indian issues. Some of the findings:

- Non-Indian citizens show a widespread posture of interest in and support for Indian issues, though amid an environment that is relatively uninformed.
- A positive link exists between personal familiarity with Indians and support for Indian issues. Familiarity most often is based on patronization of vendors and services on Indian reservation land. Some people believe that it is unfair to Indians to take advantages of their untaxed goods and services because outsiders don't deserve them.
- The concept of treaties evokes two responses: (1) that they should be respected; (2) that perhaps they should be updated.
- Likewise, the concept of sovereignty yields two opinions: (1) that Indian self-government should be respected; (2) that the state should be able to intervene for the good of the larger public.
- Peripheral issues such as the establishment and management of gaming venues sometimes cloud the more central issues of treaty obligations and sovereignty rights.

The next part of the semester-long study was a survey of 426 adult respondents in Western New York; 87% were from Erie, Niagara and Monroe Counties (which comprise the Buffalo, Niagara Falls and Rochester metropolitan areas). The study achieved a 95% confidence level for a 4.75 plus-or-minus margin of error. This polling echoed the general support observed in the focus groups and added the following specifics.

- Current public opinion seems decidedly pro-Indian on many of the issues investigated through these research projects, particularly respect for treaty provisions.

- Concurrently, public opinion seems decidedly against some of the positions proposed or taken by state government on many of the tax-related issues. Surprisingly absent from the research findings was any significant we-all-should-pay-taxes notion. Additionally, the feeling was strong that, if sales on Reservation lands were to be taxed, tribal governments should receive the tax revenues.
- Gender is not a significant factor in support or rejection of what would commonly be considered a pro-Indian position on various issues.
- Surprisingly, neither is political leaning a significant factor in most situations. At least two-thirds of political liberals, moderates and conservatives each supported the notion that treaty provisions prevent state taxation of all sales on Indian lands.
- Predictably, higher levels of education are associated with greater support for Indian issues, though not at a significant level. But even people with lower educational achievement were in the majority with support for Indian issues.
- Ethnicity is not a significant factor in support of Indian issues. An exception to this generality is that there is notably more support for maintaining treaties in their original form among ethnic minorities (56%) than among Caucasians (48%).
- Age is not a serious dividing point in support for Indian issues, with significant support throughout each age group. Continuing availability of untaxed sales to non-Indians is favored by people under thirty years old (83%) only slightly more than those thirty to forty-five years (77%) and those over forty-five years old (75%). Additionally, persons over age forty-five years were slightly more likely to support keeping treaties in their original form rather than updating them.
- However, age is a potential factor, since younger people reported having less information about Indian issues, though no less support for Indian issues. Concurrently, younger people expressed openness to knowing more about Indians.

Finally, the students conducted a content analysis of five daily metropolitan newspapers in Upstate New York: Albany, Buffalo, Rochester, Syracuse and Watertown. The study focused mainly on the then-current public policy issue of the state's efforts to attempt to collect sales tax on goods sold on Indian lands.

Research coordinators at the college concluded that the study revealed a journalistic environment somewhat out of step with the generally pro-Indian public opinion observed in the previous two research projects.

The content analysis observed that newspapers are more likely to accept assertions by New York State public officials that the state has a right and ability to collect taxes on goods purchased by non-Indians on Indian lands. The most common example was that newspapers editorialized in favor of collecting the state tax.

In particular, news articles often used the explicit phrase or implicit indication that the state is "losing money" through non-collection of taxes. The study found no references in news articles to the existing counter proposition: that, because tribal lands are recognized as sovereign by federal treaty, Indians and supports assert that the state has no legal claim to tax sales on Indian lands.

The one newspaper that was most supportive of Indian sovereignty and the most consistent with a pro-Indian point of view was the *Watertown Daily News.* The study ranked that paper as "fairly neutral," while other newspapers were more consistently adopted a pro-state, anti-Indian perspective on the taxation issue. The research coordinators speculated that Watertown's proximity to the Akwesasne Mohawk Nation at Saint. Regis, the social inter-relationship between Mohawks and non-Indians in the community, and the Mohawk Nation's strong media-relations program were significant factors in that newspaper's reporting.

Zogby Research: Citizens Pro-Indian on Issues

Zogby International is a renowned opinion survey organization based in Utica, N.Y. and in Washington, D.C. It has conducted numerous polls for a prestigious list of clients: corporations such as Microsoft and Chrysler, nonprofit organizations including many hospitals and religious groups, government agencies such as the U.S. Census Bureau and the New York State Labor Department, international organizations including the United Nations, dozens of newspapers and news services, many political candidates of both major parties, and tribal entities including the Oneida Nation Indian. All this

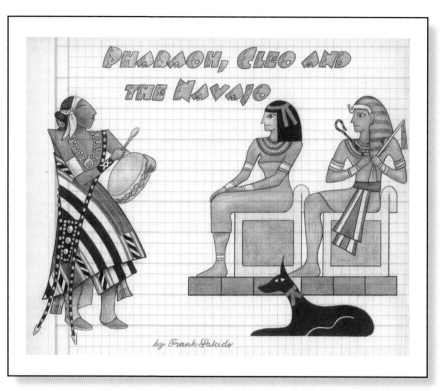

Pharaoh, Cleo and the Navajo © 2002 Frank Salcido

to say: Zogby knows its stuff.

A year after the Buffalo State students conducted their study, the Seneca Business Steering Committee commissioned Zogby to do a similar poll—bigger, on a wider scale, statistically a bit sounder than the college study. Zogby used a sample of 902 interviews of likely voters statewide—twice as big as the student survey—and achieved a margin of error of plus-or-minus 3.3%. The results between the two polls were amazingly similar.

Zogby found that 78% of New Yorkers agreed that the state and federal government "should honor the 1842 treaty," which the survey identified as the federal agreement with the Seneca Nation that protects "the lands of the Senecas within the State of New York... from all taxes and assessment for roads, highways or any other purposes." Zogby also found strong opposition (65% disagree to 34% agree) to the idea that the state should attempt to collect sales tax on items sold on Indian reservations. The poll showed support (69%) for Governor George Pataki's veto in 2003 of a bill authorizing taxation of Indian retail sales.

The Buffalo State survey had asked slightly different questions. Respondents split fifty-fifty on agreement with two statement: "Treaties between the federal government and Indian tribes should be followed as they were written" and "Treaties between the federal government and Indian tribes should be updated." But if the treaties were to be renegotiated, the largest group of respondents felt it should be initiated by Indian tribes (42%) followed by the federal government (30%) and lastly by the state government (27%).

Additionally, if there were to be a sales tax on products purchased in Indian reservations, respondents overwhelmingly said the tax revenues should go the tribal government (69%). Only 24% would give the taxes to the state, and only 7% to the federal government. The respondents in the student research project also showed an accurate—though not overwhelming—understanding of the word "sovereign" as meaning self-governing (71%) and of the word "treaty" as a legal contract with the force of law (67%).

Zogby's report concluded that Indian tribes "seem to have gained a great deal of respect from New Yorkers." The poll found that 80% of New Yorkers had a favorable view of Indian tribes in the state, and 73% had a favorable view of Indian businesspeople (compared with a 50% favorable rate for Governor Pataki and 44% favorable for the state legislature).

Zogby also claimed that the poll was particularly significant "in how broad-based the support for the Indian tribes' position is." Like the student poll, Zogby found citizen support consistent across political, age and gender categories. Zogby also reported pro-Indian sentiment in rural, suburban and metropolitan areas, and both in presumably liberal Downstate (i.e., the New York City metropolitan area) and conservative Upstate (everyplace else). All over the Empire State, it seems, New Yorkers are pro-Indian.

Another important factor in understanding these findings is that they come from state residents who, by and large, do not have frequent personal relationships with Indians. Most respondents are not regular shoppers on Indian land; the Zogby sample reported only less than a quarter of respondents actually having made any purchases from reservation vendors. Meanwhile, 62% of respondents in the Buffalo State sample said they "never or almost never" shop on Indian reservations, despite the fact that 56% said they live within twenty-five miles of a reservation.

Conclusions and Observations

Allow this author to transition to the first-person "I" for the remainder of this article. By way of disclosure, I was one of the research coordinators and lead author of the Buffalo State report; I'm also chair of the college's Communication Department and project director for the department's American Indian Policy and Media Initiative.

I have closely followed the Zogby poll—in part because of my interest in the subject matter, in part because there is an obvious ego boost in having such a prestigious research organization conduct a study similar to my own and reach essentially the same conclusions. I don't presume to suggest that Zogby copied our study or even knew of its existence; only that the consistency of findings speaks well of all parties involved.

Additionally, I have had the occasion to speak both informally with reporters and to comment more formally in workshops and presentations to newspaper staffs on how better to report on issues growing out of a diverse coverage area. Nowhere in any studies that I'm aware of nor in my own encounters with reporters (or the general citizenry, for that matter) have I found deliberate ill will, no deep-seated animosity toward American Indians. Yes, everybody is limited by her or his own background and experiences, but I don't see reporters or most other people reveling in their prejudice.

Thus I find no evidence to suggest that the journalistic shortcomings in media coverage of Indian issues that are sometimes apparent are due to lack of goodwill or integrity. Rather, I understand that journalists are busy professionals who are stretched in many different directions, sometimes lacking a depth of information, perhaps predisposed to frame stories in terms of controversy and opposing forces, and often disinclined to challenging basic assumptions of fact. What I'm hoping for is a cultural literacy among the media story tellers and message makers. Reporters take justifiable pride in fact-checking their stories. I'd like to see them give at least as priority to checking their news reports and editorial presentations for cultural sensitivity, social context and historical accuracy.

That's what I'd like to see. Unfortunately, instead I too often find that citizens and mainstream media alike seem concerned with an easy fix for economic and related policy issues. The reasoning goes like this: The state needs more money and, hey, there's some money to be had by taxing sales to non-Indian visitors to the reservation. It's a no brainer. Hence, the problem, because it really is a no brainer.

As the Buffalo State and Zogby polls show, public opinion seems solidly on the Indian side, whether the issue is taxation or land claims, casinos or archeological restitution. Underlying all these issues, it seems to me, is the concept of sovereignty—a healthy and widespread respect for the notion, sanctioned and encoded in treaties, that Indian lands are self-governing territories which exist at some degree of legal distance with the surrounding lands under the jurisdiction of the state.

Meanwhile, studies elsewhere report that the American public generally has a healthy skepticism about many of the presumed and sometimes presumptuous prerogatives of government—an attitude that also may come into play when citizens show a willingness to side with Indians against governors or state legislatures.

But the underlying factor, I think, is the fundamental knowledge that the federal and state governments have a special legal relationship with Indian entities; that Indian citizens have rights that may be different from the rights of other citizens; and that, after more than four hundred years of an admittedly uneven relationship between Indians and colonial, state, federal and territorial governments, it doesn't seem all that bad that Indians have a few special rights.

At least that seems to be the feeling among the college students whom I deal with. Most young people say they are personally acquainted with few Indians, wouldn't mind knowing more, and realize they are under-educated on various historical and contemporary issues important to the ongoing relationship between Indians and non-Indians. And I have little reason to suspect that these attitudes are not shared by the majority of people outside the academic halls.

But I see a particular need to educate reporters, editors, news directors and other media professionals. I've dedicated my life to the proposition that the communication media are tremendously important to society, that individually and collectively they can be a powerful force for good as society moves ahead in achieving tolerance, mutual understanding, and greater social/economic/political well being. But for such benefits to be achieved, we need media people who are culturally literate to the issues at hand.

Recommendations for Action

Following are some recommendations that grow out my pro-fessional and academic presumptions that (1) public policy generally results from perceived public opinion, and thus public opinion can impact public policy; (2) governors, legislators and other makers of public policy sometimes presume public opinion and public support where it may not exist; and (3) journalistic reporting often underlies such presumptions.

But first, allow me a slight detour to identify two issues of media scholarship that are useful introductions to the recommendations. Both of these issues have particular relevance to the analysis of reporting and media attention to Indian issues.

Media scholars use the phrase "agenda-setting theory of the media" to describe the notion that the media, while not necessarily telling their audiences *what to think*, can be quite successful in telling them *what to think about*. This phenomenon is in play when newspapers and other media report—or choose not to report, or under-report, or misreport certain issues important to the Indian community.

At the same time, media scholars refer to "framing" in describing the notion that the media, particularly news media, establish the parameters and ground rules for discussion of public issues. An example of such framing is the media coverage of proposals for state taxation that proceeds from the state's assertion of a right to tax sales on Indian lands, an assertion that goes unchallenged by the media because they have framed the issue with the presumption that the state is the only legitimate interpreter of its own legislative claims; they fail to even show awareness that there may be a different starting point for their reporting—and thus a different tone for the public discourse that results from their reporting.

So on to the recommendations—unsolicited, perhaps presumptuous, and focused not on what others *should* do but rather on what we *can* do ("we" being people associated with Indian interests, academic subjects or media outreach).

> **Recommendation 1**. People who shop on reservations, visit Indian cultural venues or go to tribal casinos have a higher level of support for the Indian perspective on contemporary issues than people who do not interact with Indians. We can develop public education campaigns directed toward potential non-Indians shoppers and visitors—reminding them that their support is legal and helpful to Indians and inviting them to patronize Indian businesses and cultural establishments.

> **Recommendation 2**. Despite their self-identified lack of education and information, most people seem attuned to and supportive of the pro-Indian side of many issues. Non-Indians say they want to learn more about Indian people, culture, history and economic issues. In particular, they are open to receiving accurate information about public policy issues such as treaty rights, land claims, taxation, archaeological heritage and so on. We can develop resources for provide not only for the media but for other interested members of the community.

> **Recommendation 3**. Journalists and pundits often fall into the trap of identifying issues as being either liberal or conservative, both reflecting and contributing to partisanship in public discourse. The research cited in this report shows that support for Indian issues spans political leanings. We can frame Indian issues as being above the partisan fray, such as by analyzing issues with propositions and arguments that draw on principles of both the left and the right.

Recommendation 4. Journalists pride themselves in presenting fair and full coverage of the various sides of each issue and of exploring alternative approaches to public issues. We can develop mechanisms for a consistent and authoritative presence of Indian voices in various non-Indian media outlets. Such a presence should not seek to present an artificially common Indian voice where none exists. Rather, by developing of media relations offices and training Indian spokespeople, we can more consciously and more consistently provide an Indian point of view in the public discourse.

Ronald D. Smith is a public relations professor and chair of the Communication Department at Buffalo State College (SUNY). He is Director of the American Indian Policy and Media Initiative. The full text of his research report is available at the department web site: www.AmericanIndianInitiative.buffalostate.edu.

Shaping Public Opinion: Slanted Coverage in the City of Sherrill v. Oneida Indian Nation

– By Tom Wanamaker –

Since the City of Sherrill filed its taxation lawsuit against the Oneida Nation in 1999, coverage by the two largest local dailies, the Syracuse *Post-Standard* and the Utica *Observer-Dispatch* of that litigation's progress has been timely, but not always completely accurate. The purpose here is not to accuse either paper of intentional wrongdoing—it is instead to point out that misperception of and bias against Indians are so pervasive that they commonly creep into the coverage of otherwise impartial newspaper professionals.

The Research

To access relevant articles, I used the Newsbank database, and searched the archives of both papers from January 2003 (the earliest date that the Utica paper's stories are currently available electronically) through March 2005, when the Supreme Court handed down its *Sherrill* decision. The search terms "Oneida Nation" and "Sherrill" were entered simultaneously as I sought to acquire articles with both terms in the text.

An examination of several dozen articles from these two papers reveal that the language they use, the sources they consult, and the way in which they construct their stories can frame Indian related news in general, and the Sherrill saga in particular, in ways that promote public misperception. In many of these stories, the "Indian quote" is buried in the seventh, eighth, ninth or even tenth paragraph, while the "pro-Sherrill quote" is featured within the first two or three paragraphs.

To be fair, both papers have on occasion run articles positive to the Oneidas. Both have published news stories on the Nation's Silver Covenant grants to local governments and school districts and its college scholarships for non-Indian high school seniors. Both have also touted the job-creation power of Oneida Nation business enterprises.

The Oneida Nation has sometimes refused to speak with *Post-Standard* reporters. The Nation cut off all contact for a time in 2002 and 2003, protesting what it felt was the paper's overly negative coverage. This reluctance to comment may have contributed to some of that paper's slant toward Sherrill. But on the whole, both papers could do a lot to improve the negative lean toward Indians that their articles generally contain.

More Than a Tax Case

During the time frame I examined, both papers consistently portrayed the issue in the *Sherrill* case as being solely about taxes. From Sherrill's perspective, this is true. But for the Oneida Nation, the litigation was all about protecting and asserting its sovereignty, not about avoiding taxes. The nation's refusal to pay property taxes stemmed from its belief in its own inherent tribal sovereignty over the land it owns.

Both papers give far too much credence to the so-called Upstate Citizens for Equality. A vast majority of their articles on the *Sherrill* case and on Indian issues in general contain quotes from this group, a vocal minority claiming to promote an equal tax burden for all residents of upstate New York. A look at Upstate Citizen's web sites belies this claim. All of its rhetoric is directed against Indians, the Oneida and Cayuga nations in particular, and strays widely from tax issues. The group is silent on tax issues that do not involve Indians.

For example, Upstate Citizens says nothing, on its web sites or through the media, about New York State's quasi-corrupt Empire Zone program. Originally a well-intentioned plan to spur economic development in blighted inner-city areas, the program has morphed into a loophole-ridden scheme that awards tax and utility breaks to well-connected developers for projects that create a few low paying jobs.

Destiny USA

Likewise, Upstate Citizens has been mum on Destiny USA, a controversial mega-mall and tourist destination project proposed by the Pyramid Companies in Syracuse. In return for building this ambitious project, for which it refuses to reveal a coherent design or plan, the developer seeks a thirty-year exemption from paying property taxes to the city of Syracuse.

The *Post-Standard* and the *Observer-Dispatch* interview this group's leaders solely about Indian issues, not about other obvious tax issues. Neither paper, as best as we can determine, asked Upstate Citizen's opinion on Empire Zones, Destiny, or other tax-related issues like New York's brutally high tax burden and Albany's twenty-year streak of late budgets. All of these issues would seem to lie within the group's supposed interest in promoting an equal tax burden for all. But they say nothing, and the papers don't ask.

The Hate Group

Both the National Congress of American Indians and the Oneida Nation have publicly identified Upstate Citizens for Equality as a hate group.

Although, the Syracuse and Utica papers are generally thorough in their approaches to other issues, neither paper appears to have questioned or investigated Upstate Citizen's ethnic-centered motives. Isn't the presence of an alleged hate group within a community a worthy topic for journalism? How would these papers react if other hate groups that target other racial or ethnic groups set up shop in upstate New York?

What the Post-Standard Says

A look at a few examples of published articles and editorials will offer a feel for the generally anti-Indian tone of these papers' coverage.

The *Post-Standard* published a news story under the headline "Counties bemoan Oneidas' tax-exemption" (Coin, 2003). The second sentence of this article calls the Oneida Nation's Turning Stone Casino Resort "a visible and vexing symbol of the erosion of the tax base in Madison and Oneida counties." This qualifies as inflammatory rhetoric and creates the impression that the Oneidas alone are responsible for the two counties' economic problems. If the reader reads no further, that's the gist he or she would take from this article.

By the eighth paragraph, the reporter gets around to mentioning the plethora of other tax-exempt properties owned by various non-Indian people and entities. He also discusses various other tax exemptions, but inexplicably fails to mention Empire Zones. While this article is actually a bit fairer to Indians than most, it contradicts itself before ending with a pair of inaccuracies.

The contradiction is here: After describing Turning Stone as a symbol of the declining tax base, in his third and fourth paragraphs the reporter says that tax-exempt properties comprise 35% and 25% of all property in Oneida and Madison counties. But then in the ninth paragraph, the reporter says that tribally owned land comprises merely 5% of the tax-free property in the two counties.

It is not until the eighteenth paragraph that the reporter states that "state-owned land is the single biggest category of tax exemption in Madison and Oneida counties." Why, then, is the Turning Stone cast as a "symbol" the region's declining tax base? Would it not be more accurate to lead this article with a statement like the sentence on state land, cited above, that was buried deep in the article?

Inaccuracies

The first inaccuracy is its assertion that Oneidas "do not pay" sales taxes. This is incorrect—Oneida Indians shopping at any off-reservation retailer pay the same sales taxes as does everyone else. What the author was probably referring to is the fact that Oneida-owned retail businesses do not collect state sales taxes because the nation does not view itself as an agent of New York State. Properly wording and explaining this issue might help to correct the common misperception that "Indians don't pay taxes."

The second comes in the last paragraph when a thirty-two acre parcel of land on Route 46 south of the city of Oneida is described as the Nation's "original" territory. Actually, the Oneida Nation's original ancestral territory stretched from the St. Lawrence River to what is now the Pennsylvania border, and from around Chittenango in the west to the Utica/Rome area in the east. The thirty-two acre tract was the only land that New York was unable to take away from the nation.

Framed

In early November 2004, the Supreme Court announced that it would hear arguments in the *City of Sherrill v. Oneida Indian Nation* case. On November 12, the *Post-Standard* published a story that began with the following sentence: "The city of Sherrill has a date with the U.S. Supreme Court." This lead immediately laid out the story's bias— framing the story this way paints Sherrill as the "good guys" and the Oneidas as the "bad guys" (Coin 2004).

The article quotes the chairman of the Madison County Board of Supervisors, Rocco DiVeronica, a staunch opponent of Oneida sovereignty. It also quotes Sherrill's lawyer, Ira Sacks. But there are no quotes from the Oneida Nation—not even a notation asserting that they declined to comment, and why.

The article frames the case solely from the city's perspective, while asking questions to which the newspaper should already have known the answers.

It asks if the land is tribal, and if that means it's not taxable. The reporters should have known that the U.S. Supreme Court ruled in 1985 that this land was tribal. Could the land have really been reservation land if it was established by the state of New York? They should have known that the U.S. guaranteed the reservation in the *1784,* Treaty of Canandaigua. Didn't the 1938, Treaty of Buffalo Creek disband the Oneida reservation? Again, the Supreme Court already ruled that the reservation was not disbanded. Does the land remain tribal if the Oneida cease to exist as a tribal nation? That's the wishful thinking of hate groups.

The Oneida Nation has never ceased to exist since its 1784 treaty with the U.S., and there is no reason to think it ever will.

Indian Country

Another problem with this article is its use of the term "Indian Country." A popular phrase in Native American communities and media as observable in the newspapers *Indian Country Today* and *News From Indian Country*. Indian Country can be defined in various ways to imply everything from reservations to urban Indian communities to the millions of acres that the U.S. took from tribes. The phrase has no place in a news articles about a Supreme Court case involving a specific tribal nation and specific lands.

The newspaper reports further failed to explore important national implications of this case.

Unlike the city's argument, which basically sought to distract the Court by rehashing old issues, the Oneidas presented a novel legal theory. They argued that because Congress never disestablished their reservation, the nation continues to hold aboriginal title to the land. By acquiring property within the old reservation boundaries from willing sellers, the tribe unites fee title with aboriginal title and is thus able to reassert its sovereign control over the lands guaranteed it by the federal government.

Missing the News

Yet the *Post-Standard* apparently does not see such an innovative argument as newsworthy. Instead the article reports only that the Oneida Nation "argues" that the land is part of its reservation and that it "claims" that the state illegally acquired the reservation lands. At the same time the newspaper failed to report that knowledgeable historians and legal scholars agreed with the Oneida's interpretation. Thus *Post-Standard* acted like a surrogate prosecutor. But in failing to properly and fairly summarize the nation's judicial stance, the newspaper did its readers a serious disservice. By presenting the *Sherrill* case in such a one-sided manner, the newspaper created a condition in which readers will automatically dismiss the Oneida Nation's stance without ever being exposed to it, much less gaining the opportunity to understand it.

On March 30, 2005, after the Supreme Court's announcement of its decision in *Sherrill*, the *Post-Standard* published what it called the "official reaction" (*Post-Standard* 2005). But the paper failed miserably in offering a broad spectrum of reactions—every person quoted has long been on record as opposing the Oneida land claim, including state Assemblymen Bill Magee and David Townsend, and State Senator David Valesky. By labeling these peoples' and other's statements of "common sense," "vindication," and "positive development," as somehow "official," the paper gives undue credence to the notion that this erroneous decision is justified.

What about Governor George Pataki or Senator Hilary Clinton? Why are there no comments from the Oneida Nation, the Native

American Rights Fund, the United South and Eastern Tribes, the U.S. Bureau of Indian affairs or the National Congress of the American Indian? Why are no Indian law experts included? Are such reactions any less official? What is so official about a bunch of people who are generally known to be unsympathetic to the Indian cause?

After All

"Consider This," an editorial published in the *Post-Standard* (2005), discusses federal Judge David Hurd's ruling that Madison County cannot foreclose on Oneida land for non-payment of property taxes. It states that Hurd's ruling means that "the property in question is tribal land after all."

After all? In *Sherrill*, the Supreme Court said that the Oneida Nation could not "unilaterally revive its ancient sovereignty" over land re-acquired from willing sellers. It did not rule on the legitimacy of Oneida claims to the land. The court simply refused to provide a remedy for the nation and instead passed the buck to the Interior Department, which will rule on the Oneida's land-trust application. With the words "after all," "unilaterally" and "ancient" the editorial board reveals that it may not comprehend what the *Sherrill* decision really means, which is that the court strayed into "legal territory that belongs to Congress," as Justice Stevens correctly said in his dissent. "Only Congress has the power to diminish or disestablish a tribe's reservation."

It's not tribal land "after all"—it's tribal land because Congress never said it wasn't. But the Syracuse paper failed to explore this angle.

The Utica Observer-Dispatch Reports

Utica *Observer-Dispatch* did no better. Following are but a few examples.

In a editorial, the *Observer-Dispatch* states that "the Oneidas say that New York state illegally took some [land] from them ..." (2004a). It's not that the Oneidas *say* so; what's important is that the Supreme Court ruled as such in 1985. A more responsibly written editorial would have noted this fact (which is probably filed somewhere in the newspaper's library) rather than simply framing the issue as an assertion by the Oneidas rather than an opinion from the highest court in United States.

In its end-of-the-year summary of top stories, the *Observer-Dispatch* failed to mention any of the Oneida Nation's lower court victories in the *Sherrill* case (2004b).

In its headlines and leads, the *Observer-Dispatch* consistently referred to Sherrill's status as the smallest city in New York State, as if to paint Sherrill as a David against Goliath of the Oneida Nation. Comparing the size of the two entities serves no purpose, as they are not analogous in any way. But this was done repeatedly in the run-up to the hearing in January 2005 and after the decision was announced in late March of that year.

In 2004, the U.S. Census Bureau estimated the City of Sherrill's population to be 3,126 or the least populous entity in New York State with a city-style government. The Oneida Indian Nation is a federally recognized Indian nation with approximately 1,000 enrolled members, although its business enterprises employ some 5,000 people, a vast majority of whom are non-Indians. What good does it do to compare the size of these two entities? It's akin to comparing a banana to a turnip.

No Sherrill Residents

The *Observer-Dispatch* published another irresponsible article headlined "Sherrill tense in advance of court arguments" (Karch 2005). The story's two quotes come from people who don't even live in Sherrill, but reside instead in Oneida. The first source inexplicably states that people are afraid of repercussions from the Oneidas and that the nation owns "every corner in the city of Oneida." The second statement is patently false, and the first is rumor-mongering of the basest kind. What repercussions? Why were no Sherrill residents quoted? If Sherrill is tense, as the headline implies, the reporter should get quotes from people or members of the police force in Sherrill.

Once again, emphasis is placed on the idea that the Oneida Nation claims that its land was wrongfully taken from it, rather than the fact that the Supreme Court ruled it so in 1985. And, other than a brief quote from a Nation spokesman, a majority of the other quotes in the story are negative toward the Nation. In addition the *Observer-Dispatch* quotes not one, but two members of the Upstate Citizens for Equality group.

Interestingly, Upstate Citizens is described in the article as a "landowner's advocacy group," even though two paragraphs later, the reporter mentions that Upstate Citizens is fighting against the nation's casino compact. What does this have to do with landowners? Why didn't the reporter ask?

Why does the *Observer-Dispatch* place quotation marks around the nation's identification of Upstate Citizens as a hate group? The paper might be wise to investigate its source rather than simply dismissing the predominant Native opinion. Why doesn't the paper ask Upstate Citizens' prominent spokesmen about other taxation issues in New York.

The Hate Group Quoted

There are numerous historians, lawyers and others in New York and the U.S. who possess expert knowledge. Yet such people are rarely quoted, while Upstate Citizens' talking heads pop up with astounding frequency. These supposed experts offers distorted facts to suit its agenda and makes a lot of noise in hopes of getting its agenda to prevail.

In reporting on Indian-related issues, reporters at both the *Post-Standard* and the *Observer-Dispatch* see fit to seek the Upstate Citizens for Equality's perspective as they apparently fail to establish contact with legitimate, knowledgeable experts who understand law, taxation and sovereignty as they relate to Indians. This one-sided reporting results in a serious failure to present the truth.

As the discerning reader with a talent for reading between the lines will note, both of these Central New York dailies consistently fail to report Indian issues fairly. Next time you read a newspaper story about an Indian issue, look at how the issues are framed and who the writer quotes. For instance, this alarming pattern followed the aforementioned reporter to her next newspaper, the *Everett Herald* in Washington, where again in 2007 she quoted hate groups.

The Aftermath

By any measure, the Supreme Court's *Sherrill* ruling was a disaster for the Oneidas, one that will surely resonate loudly throughout tribal nations in the U.S. for decades to come. In rejecting the Oneida attempt to reassert its inherent control over ancestral territories, the

Court pushed the Oneida Nation into a new fight—that of having to surrender title to the federal government, after first convincing the federal Bureau of Indian Affairs to take the land into trust.

In local newspaper coverage of the first round of BIA hearings, which took place in early 2006 in Oneida and Madison counties, we have already begun to see how the Syracuse and Utica papers will frame these discussions. Upstate Citizens for Equality and negative local politicians continue to dominate coverage, despite them representing the minority opinion at both meetings.

Whenever somebody makes the outrageous claim that there is no basis or justification for the land-trust process, neither paper cites the *Sherrill* decision, which specifically directs the Oneidas to apply for trust status.

Tom Wanamaker has reported extensively on American Indian economics, policies and gaming. His column "Let the Games Begin" about the tribal casino industry appears in Indian Country Today, *which is an enterprise of the Oneida Nation.*

References

Coin, G. 2003, June 1. "Counties bemoan Oneidas' tax-exemption—Madison and Oneida county officials say nation should contribute to tax base," Syracuse *Post-Standard*, p. B1.

Coin, G. 2004, Nov. 12. "Sherrill, Oneidas get date for court—U.S. Supreme Court justices will hear oral arguments in city tax case on Jan. 11," Syracuse *Post-Standard*, p. B1.

Karch, K. J. 2005, Jan. 9. "Sherrill tense in advance of court arguments," Utica *Observer-Dispatch*, p. 1A.

Observer-Dispatch (Utica). 2004a, July 1. "Land claim" (editorial), p. 11A.

Observer-Dispatch (Utica). 2004b, Dec. 26. "Issues culminated in year's top stories" (unattributed), p. 1A.

Post-Standard (Syracuse). 2004, Nov. 1. "Consider this" (editorial), p. A12.

Post-Standard (Syracuse). 2005, Mar. 30. "Official reaction to the Supreme Court decision on Sherrill v. Oneida Nation" (unattributed), p. A9.

The Enlightened Racist
and the Anti-Gaming Movement

– by Michael I. Niman –

Contemporary American racism is not cut and dry. It's not as if only those who don hoods and burn crosses or raise Nazi salutes are racists. "Enlightened" racism is much more complicated. Today's typical racist rhetorically abhors racism. Author Gloria Yamato writes that charges of racism drive "usually tranquil white liberals wild when they get called on it." Racism, in today's American society, is, quite frankly, out of vogue. Still, it's persistent.

Modern Racism

Modern racism divides oppressed peoples into categories of "good ones" and "bad ones." The good ones are those folks who, against the odds of a gamed system, have prospered. Such success stories are often spotlighted in the media—being newsworthy because of their relative rarity in the media. For the enlightened racist, these narratives serve as further proof that the "bad ones" have only failed because of their own shortcomings. Absent in the simplistic analysis offered by these twin images is any reference to systemic racism that condemns historically disadvantaged peoples to poor schools, poor housing and poor health. And of course there is no recognition of the fact that so many members of the dominant culture were born into privilege. This privilege includes being born into a family with college educated parents and attending well funded schools, being networked with people who can help you find jobs, or even living in a community where there are jobs to be had. This privilege also includes being born into a group that is not persistently suffering from various form of racial or ethnic discrimination.

Racism is less about skin color or any other physical marker than about the power of the dominant group. It constructs and supports privilege, or political and economic, advantage. And of course where there is privilege there is oppression since nobody can enjoy privilege without someone else suffering a lack of privilege. With racism, one group gains and maintains power over another group.

The United States was built on a foundation of racism. This is an ugly reality we need to face up to. Across the Americas, European invaders slaughtered or assimilated Native peoples based on the supposed superiority of European culture and religions over what we now know were more sustainable Native cultures. Employing words like "savage" and "primitive," so called "modern" and "civilized" cultures unleashed a historically unprecedented holocaust upon the hemisphere. This racism was continued as modern America was built with enslaved African laborers and indentured workers, primarily from China and Ireland. And it continues today in various forms as the dominant groups in America maintain their economic and political dominance over traditionally subjugated groups, such as Native Americans—including those who emigrated north from Latin America.

To fully understand the scope of this racism, it is useful to examine how community activists in the United States are manipulated into supporting racist movements targeting Native American rights and the sovereign political identities of Native nations. In New York State, for example, community activists are fanning the flames in the U.S. and Canada's ongoing war against the Haudenosaunee (Iroquois Six Nations).

In the consciousness of most Americans and Canadians, these wars are relegated to the realm of history, yet flare-ups are now occurring across Six Nations territory. Armed Ontario government forces spent most of 2006 engaged in a standoff with residents and supporters of the Six Nations Grand River Reserve over contested land where a local developer is attempting to build a subdivision in the municipality of Caledonia.

As the conflict at Six Nations heated up in the summer of 2006, officers from the U.S. Border Patrol and Bureau of Alcohol, Tobacco,

Firearms and Explosives mysteriously appeared north of the border in Caledonia, where Native protesters commandeered their unmarked car. In doing so they made the U.S. presence into a news story. Canadian media reported that U.S. officials were ostensibly in Canada to "observe" how Canadian police dealt with Native protesters.

One hundred and thirty miles to the southeast, Central New York's Upstate Citizens for Equality is using U.S. courts to challenge Haudenosaunee sovereignty—including that of the Oneida land where that Nation's Turning Stone Casino is located.

On both sides of the border, officials from the powerful immigrant-settled states impose their laws and courts upon the Haudenosaunee nations when settling territorial disputes. The U.S. and Canada, however, never conquered the sovereign Haudenosaunee nations. Haudenosaunee territorial sovereignty is guaranteed by internationally recognized peace treaties signed in good faith with the U.S. and Canada and with Canada's former landlords. The U.S. in particular recognized this sovereignty before it gained savvy as a conquering power, hence it failed to create many of the paper loopholes it subsequently used to attack Native sovereignty in western North America.

Sovereignty

This uncompromising sovereignty is the legal basis that allows the Seneca Nation, historically part of the Haudenosaunee Confederacy, to build, for example, casinos on its land—including its newly re-acquired Buffalo Creek territory adjacent to downtown Buffalo, New York. For U.S. citizens, the emergence of sovereign foreign territory in the middle of Buffalo may be a difficult concept to swallow. This retaking of lost territory was made possible by a rather recent piece of congressional legislation articulating a deal with the Seneca Nation allowing the U.S. city of Salamanca to remain on their Allegheny reservation in exchange for recognizing Seneca rights to annex property that they purchase within their historic land claim area.

This deal poses a real challenge for activists who oppose casino gambling. As independent sovereign states, the historically Haudenosaunee nations on the U.S. side of the border, have a right like other sovereign nations around the globe to write their own laws, and to decide internally whether, for example, casino gambling will be legal or illegal in their lands. The challenge then, is how to oppose casino plans by a neighboring nation without opposing the right of that nation to exist? Or put simply, how to be anti-casino without being anti-Indian—how to oppose casinos without supporting the centuries-old war against the Haudenosaunee?

Of course, this is possible if seldom practiced. People oppose bingo without opposing the Catholic Church. They organize against state lotteries and state-run off track betting parlors without opposing the existence of states. Ultimately, with intelligence, anti-casino forces could oppose casinos without opposing Native nations' sovereignty or Native peoples in general.

Western New York, however, is witnessing an ugly courtship between anti-casino and anti-Indian political forces. In June of 2006, for example, Coalition Against Gaming in New York Chair Joel Rose, a community activist, e-mailed a message entitled "Good News on Turning Stone" to his membership listserv. In it, he celebrated a New York State Court of Appeals decision against Cayuga and Oneida land claims. This court victory does not stand up to the muster of international law, which Haudenosaunee leaders consider the proper jurisdiction for such disputes.

Rose was excited because the case could eventually lead to the closing of the Oneida Turning Stone Casino in Central New York. If so, and if the Oneidas refuse to comply, it could also lead to some form of armed takeover of Oneida land—what elsewhere in the world we call war.

Anyone cheering such a court victory is cheering the unilateral imposition of New York State law on a sovereign nation—much like the invasion of Kuwait by Iraq which led to the first Gulf War. While this imposition could lead to the closure of a casino, it would be like nuking a city to kill one fugitive. The casino would be closed—but only after the Oneida's land was occupied, and their identity as a sovereign nation eradicated. This kind of violation of U.S. treaties and international law is nothing that any person should celebrate.

These same activists never called for invading Canada to shut down Canadian casinos, even though the Canadian casinos are much closer to their home base of Buffalo, N.Y. Sure, this idea is ludicrous. But why isn't it just as ludicrous to ask the New York and United States governments to do exactly that to the Senecas? Is it acceptable just because it's possible? Because we're strong and they're weak? Because we've done that to Native nations so many times before?

I wrote to Rose, asking him why he reveled in the possible closure of one nation's casino 150 miles from his home, while giving a pass to nearby Canadian casinos just across the Niagara River. Rose responded, writing that his group tries to "focus on what we can reasonably hope to have some influence over, and that does not include the actions of the government of Ontario."

Rose went on to explain that I "misunderstood the legal status of the Indian nations. They are sovereign," he argued, "but the meaning of sovereign is something different than the sovereignty of truly foreign nations such as Canada." He based his argument on the fact that there are Indian individuals who are also U.S. citizens, who pay U.S. taxes and who vote in U.S. elections. More Canadian and Mexican transplants fit into that category then Haudenosaunee, but I've never heard that argument used to negate Canadian or Mexican sovereignty, which is grounded in the same legal precepts as Haudenosaunee sovereignty. There are also Haudenosaunee who have refused dual-citizenship, travel on their own passports, never vote in U.S. elections and don't pay taxes.

The question which I posed in the beginning is, when do anti-casino activists cross the line to racism? Is it when they overlook their own U.S. federal law concerning Native tribes and nations, which begins with treaties, which the U.S. Constitution recognize as the supreme law of the land? Is it when they foster the same old states' rights arguments used in the 1960s to support an American Apartheid known as segregation to battle the very existence of Native nations? Is it when they lose the ability to see Indians as having rights to keep and interpret their own history? Is it when they assume that their government has a paternal right to arrange Indian affairs as it sees fit? Is it when they brand Indians as criminals for following their own laws, many of which pre-exist the state of New York and the United States? Is it when they interpret historic Haudenosaunee treaty rights to sovereignty to be somehow less than those of Canadians or Mexicans?

Cayuga: Not Just a Name

Locally, the map of Central and Western New York was drawn by military leaders who, after the American Revolution, sent the U.S. Army into Haudenosaunee (Iroquois) territory to annihilate Native populations. Cayuga Lake, for example, is circled by historic markers denoting Cayuga villages and orchards burned during the Sullivan Campaign of 1779. Then there are the markers commemorating the first homes built by white men, right in the wake of that campaign. Armed with the ideology of racism and employing the practice of ethnic cleansing, this was about power and political advantage. In short, it was a land grab—with mass murder as its tool.

This is what sets racism against Native Americans apart from racism targeted against other oppressed groups. The U.S. Commission on Civil Rights, in its 1981 report, *Indian Tribes: A Continuing Quest for Survival*, noted that the development of civil rights issues for Native Americans evolved in reverse of the pattern for other oppressed groups in North America. "Politically," the report states, other groups "started with nothing and had attempted to gain a voice in the existing economic and political structure. Indians started with everything and have gradually lost much of what they had to an advancing alien civilization." This pattern of losing power and wealth has victimized Native populations in North America, forcing most Indian nations and tribes into poverty. Enlightened racists have subsequently blamed Indians for that poverty—often with no understanding of this history or its consequences.

In recent decades as Native nations, including those of the Haudenosaunee, regained political power, land base and economic stability, the anti-Indian movement has bloomed, almost humorously characterizing white America as an underdog beside Native nations.

Hence, in the villages of Union Springs and Cayuga, N.Y., on the shores of Cayuga Lake, in Cayuga County, we now have an almost all-white group of people oxymoronically called the "Upstate Citizens for Equality," who have formed to oppose a sovereign Cayuga presence. In essence, what the group is doing, is struggling to maintain its own political advantage over the people who historically had jurisdiction over the land that the group's members now claim as their own.

In 2002, Upstate Citizens branched out to form a Western New York (Buffalo) Chapter to combat Seneca land claims and eventually join forces with anti-casino activists—in effect attempting to co-opt the anti-gaming forces into the anti-sovereignty movement. (Ironically, their office is located on Indian Church Road in the Buffalo suburb of West Seneca.) After I wrote a column for Buffalo's weekly *ArtVoice*, asking the question, "when do well intentioned activists cross the line to racism?," Joel Rose, a leader of Buffalo's anti-casino movement, responded, writing a letter arguing, "We are not racists: I have never uttered a racist word or expression." Rose went on to defend the Upstate Citizens for Equality, arguing, "UCE has based its position on the distinctly non-racist notion that we should all be playing by the same rules."

The problem with this argument is that the rules UCE argues we all have to play by aren't mutually agreed upon—they are the rules that white society imposed on the Haudenosaunee during the Sullivan Campaign. In his letter, Rose goes on to describe Haudenosaunee territory as "islands of sovereignty in the middle of a modern nation." Now, while Rose isn't donning a hood or shouting epithets, he is arguing the notion that Indians who live in the here and now are somehow not part of the modern world, and that hence, they have to play by rules that a so-called modern nation imposes upon them. This is the same rhetorical argument white society used to justify genocide and ethnocide against supposed "savage," "primitive" or "uncivilized" Indian nations in the seventeenth and eighteenth centuries.

What UCE and Rose are arguing for is not equality—it's the maintenance of a power dynamic that privileges non-natives at the cost of disempowering Native nations. And of course, Rose's statement begs the question, if Native nations are not modern nations, then what exactly is Rose suggesting they are? And if this assumption justifies their disempowerment, then is it racist?

The Final Solution

Upstate Citizens for Equality and the anti-casino Coalition Against Gaming in New York tie together though their leadership, with Daniel Warren serving as Chair of the Western New York Chapter of Upstate Citizens and as a Director of the Coalition. Warren also owns the Internet domains for both groups' web sites, listing the Upstate Citizens' chapter office in West Seneca, New York, as the administrator's address for the Coalition's web site. In a letter responding to my above-mentioned *ArtVoice* column, Warren also identifies Upstate Citizens as a member organization of the coalition against gaming.

What is interesting here is that while Upstate Citizens is anti-tribal sovereignty, and hence, one could argue, anti-Haudenosaunee, since Haudenosaunee identity and political power are entwined with sovereignty, Upstate Citizens is not against gaming. And interestingly enough neither is Coalition chair Daniel Warren. He's just against Native nations controlling casinos. In his letter, Warren wrote that he supports "either the rescission or full legalization of gambling, but not the granting of a monopoly [to Native nations]."

So if Warren, a director of the anti-casino coalition, is not against casinos, then what exactly is he against? According to Warren, Upstate Citizens supports "an expeditious and final resolution of all Indian land claims." The Niagara Frontier Chapter of Upstate Citizens echoes this call in their mission statement. It's alarming to see anyone calling for "final resolutions" to any ethnic conflict since the phrase echoes the well-known Nazi "final solution" calling for the annihilation through genocide of the Jewish people. Nazis came up with their so-called solution only after first discussing the forced relocation of Jews onto reservations in Madagascar. Upstate Citizens' idea of a final solution is the ultimate negation of Native sovereignty—a sovereignty that has until now survived five hundred years of oppression and is integral to Haudenosaunee and Seneca identity.

It's also interesting to point out that Haudenosaunee nations don't have the monopoly on gambling that Warren describes. New York, like most other U.S. states, is now replete with "racinos," off-track betting parlors, keno, lotto and lotteries, bingo etc. In addition New Yorkers patronize casinos in neighboring states and Canadian provinces. In his letter, coalition chair Rose answered my question as to why his organization focuses just on Indian-run casinos, writing that, for example, "Bingo generally involves low stakes and has low potential for addiction." Bingo also, however, often involves low-income gamblers according to a 2003 report by the Texas Lottery Commission, for whom losing low stakes can be as economically disastrous as a middle-class person losing high stakes at a casino. By focusing on Indian gaming and not gambling in general, by joining forces with Upstate Citizens, and by admitting leadership that is not opposed to gambling, the Coalition Against Gaming in New York has crossed the line from being an anti-casino group to being an anti-Indian group.

The issue always comes back among anti-Indian hate groups to sovereignty. Niagara University Hospitality Management Professor Steve Siegel, for example, in a cover story he wrote for Buffalo's weekly *ArtVoice*, explains that an Indian-run casino at Buffalo Creek would have an unfair advantage over other businesses.

To make his point, Siegel echoes an old anti-sovereignty argument,

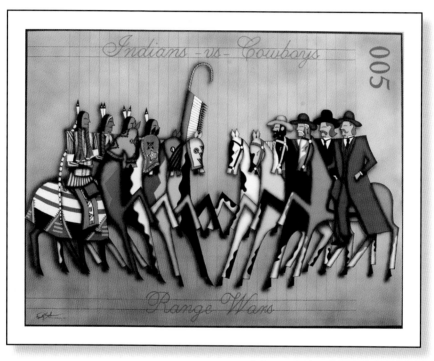

Indians vs. Cowboys © 2003 Frank Salcido

explaining that U.S. federal, state and local agencies will not have authority to regulate Seneca activities. He writes "those who feel they were discriminated against by Indian employers" will not be able to file a complaint with the U.S. National Labor Relations Board. He goes on to explain that victims of sexual harassment in Indian businesses "cannot sue the Seneca Nation for lost wages or psychological damages in [U.S.] federal court." The same holds true, however, for workers in Canadian casinos—or any businesses outside of the U.S. for that matter. This is sovereignty. Workers are protected, or not protected, by the laws of the nations where they work—with some nations having stronger or weaker worker protection laws then the U.S.

It's interesting that Siegel, whose article attacks sovereignty but not the idea of casinos, chose to discuss hypothetical sexual harassment and discrimination by Indians. By doing so he is continuing an old reconstruction-era tradition of terrifying white audiences with images of emancipated black males sexually victimizing helpless white female victims. This was an underlying theme, for example, in *Birth of a Nation*, the first epic-length motion picture made.

Siegel goes on to list all of the areas, ranging from health permits and inspections, to music and liquor licenses, where Native businesses will be unregulated. Absent in the professor's analysis, however, is the fact that the Senecas, as a sovereign nation, are the ones who regulate and adjudicate all of these issues as they see fit—just like their sovereign Canadian counterparts across the Niagara river—without needing paternalistic oversight from their U.S. neighbors.

This is what enrages Native peoples as racist—the unquestioned notion that sovereign Indian nations are not competent to manage their own affairs. This idea of Native peoples needing paternal oversight was the justification used by U.S. administrations for imposing Bureau of Indian Affairs control over Native resources, primarily in Western North America. These officials often then looted Native resources, giving sweetheart deals to white-owned mineral and energy extraction companies. As a result, since the inception of the Bureau of Indian Affairs (BIA), Native nations have lost over 137 billion dollars in assets and potential revenues due to BIA corruption and mismanagement.

Yes, potential victims may not be able to sue the Seneca Nation under U.S. federal labor laws, as Siegel argues. But what Siegel doesn't mention, is that they can sue in Seneca Peacemakers Court—in the Nation where the infraction occurred. Siegel apparently doesn't understand or respect the long-standing traditions of sovereignty and justice in Native America. This argument that Native tribes and nations can't govern themselves is part and parcel of the colonizer's fabrication, a fabrication that the great white fathers of the U.S. and Canada used to bring Native nations to the brink of annihilation through the methodology of ethnic cleansing. Here the enlightened racist, the one who twists the language and the law to outlaw indigenous America, shows his face.

Michael I. Niman *is an assistant professor of communications at Buffalo State College. He is a member of the Minority Media and Telecommunications Council brain trust and a member of the Steering Committee of the Union for Democratic Communications.*

References

Avalon Project at Yale Law School. 2006. "Treaties Between the United States and Native Americans" (online database). http://www.yale.edu/lawweb/avalon/ntreaty/ntreaty.htm, accessed July 26, 2006.

Campbell, Christopher P. 1998. "Beyond Employment Diversity: Rethinking Contemporary Racist News Representations." In *Cultural Diversity and the U.S. Media*, Yahya R. Kamalipour and Theresa Carilli, eds. Albany: State University of New York Press, pp. 51–64.

Canadian Press Newswire. 2006, June 19. "Six Nations Protesters Deny Bunker Being Built at Site in Caledonia, Ont."

Hemsworth, Wade. 2006, June 16. "Two societies, two very different approaches," *Hamilton Spectator*, p. A4.

Jensen, Robert. 2005. *The Heart of Whiteness: Confronting Race, Racism, and White Privilege.* San Francisco: City Lights.

Jhally, Sut, and Justin Lewis. 1992. *Enlightened Racism: The Cosby Show, Audiences, and the Myth of the American Dream.* Boulder: Westview Press.

Johnson, Allan G. 2001. *Privilege, Power and Difference.* Mountain View, CA: Mayfield Publishing.

Lui, Meizhu, Barbara Robles, Betsy Leondar-Write, Rose Brewer, and Rebecca Adamson. 2006. *The Color or Wealth: The Story Behind the U.S. Racial Wealth Divide.* New York: The New Press.

Monteiro, Liz. 2006, June 21. "Caledonia Dispute Succeeds in Giving Aboriginals 'a Voice,'" *Guelph Mercury,* p. A5.

Nelson, Marissa. 2006, June 16. "Our Agent was in Vehicle: U.S. Agency; ATF Staffer in Caledonia to Share Intelligence, Spokesman Says," *Hamilton Spectator,* p. 15.

Niman, Michael. 2006, June 15. "Anti-Casino or Anti-Indian: When do Activists Cross the Line?" *ArtVoice,* pp.16–17.

Rollings, Willard Hughes. 2004. "Indians and Christianity. In A Companion to American Indian History." In *Companion to American Indian History,* Philip J. Deloria and Neil Salisbury, eds. Malden, MA: Blackwell, pp. 121–138.

Rose, Joel. 2006, July 20. "Letters to *ArtVoice*: We Are Not Racists," *ArtVoice,* pp. 4–5.

Siegel, Steve. 2006, July 19. "The Odds Against," *ArtVoice,* pp. 11–14.

Texas Lottery Commission. 2003. "Texas Charitable Bingo Player Survey: Demographics and Participation." http:// www.txlottery.org/bingo/ pdfs/2003_bingofinalreport.doc, accessed August 2, .

Upstate Citizens for Equality. 2006. "Niagara Frontier Chapter Mission Statement." http://www.upstate-citizens.org/nfc-mission.htm, accessed July 24, .

U.S. Commission on Civil Rights. 1981, June. "Indian Tribes: A Continuing Quest for Survival."

Warren, Daniel T. 2006. "Response to Mr. Niman's Article, Anti-Casino or Anti-Indian?" Speakupwny.com. http://www.speakupwny.com/article_ 2743.shtml accessed July 26, .

Wellman, David. 1977. *Portraits of White Racism.* Cambridge: Cambridge University Press.

Yamato, Gloria. 1998. "Something About the Subject Makes it Hard to Name." In *Race, Class and Gender: An Anthology*, 3rd ed, Margaret L. Andersen and Patricia Hill Collins, eds. Belmont, CA: Wadsworth Press, pp. 89–93.

Zremski, Jerry. 2002a, May 9. "Casinos Would Extend Senecas' Sovereignty," *Buffalo News*, p. A1.

Zremski, Jerry. 2002b, Nov. 13. "Senecas Get to Buy Casino Land; Interior Secretary's Ruling Removes Last Federal Regulatory Obstacle," *Buffalo News*, p. A1.

Introduction to Three Pieces About Native Peoples, Race and Government Policy

The American news media doesn't know what to do with race-related stories.

In 2006 and 2007 a series of events have propelled issues concerning indigenous Americans into a news media unprepared for complex stories that fall out of the stereotypical racial boundaries.

The confusion is that most so-called racial minorities in the U.S. identify themselves along racial lines. Native Americans don't. We identify ourselves first as citizens of tribal nations, a status that is primarily political.

These citizens, commonly called members of one or another tribe, are based on lineage that leads to a specific family within a specific nation. Generally this family and its nation lead to specific geography on which the individual's ancestors lived at the time of first contact with the colonial nation America.

Unlike racial groups whether African American or white European, Native American identity cannot be claimed by a simple say so. This confuses not only journalists, but also political leaders who have tried to turn the right wing charge of "race-based" or "racially defined enclaves" against federal agencies and programs serving Native America. It has been the job of Native leaders to explain that we are nations, and individually citizens and descendants of nations to whom the U.S. promised a variety of services and protections at the time when our nations signed treaties ceding collectively the continent.

Further evidence that Native nations are not a racial group comes from Alaska Native corporations in which through inheritance and gifting not all shareholders are Alaska Natives, and also from a variety of tribal nations in which white and black people without Native lineage were historically incorporated and their descendants remain citizens of some modern tribal nations.

It's in that context that we turn to the Cherokee-Freedmen debate of 2007, and later the defeat in the U.S. Senate on June 8, 2006 of the Akaka bill, which would have extended the federal policy of self-governance and self-determination formally to Native Hawaiians.

The Cherokee Nation

The news of the Cherokee Nation vote to expel black Freedmen from its citizenry broke in the media like a storm in March 2007. The American Indian Policy and Media Initiative's Ronald D. Smith moved quickly to survey news coverage.

The survey, which follows, showed that media was responding to the Cherokee's internal debate in classic black civil right terms without understanding, or apparently without trying to understand, the Cherokee Nation's right to determine who its citizens are. The *New York Times* editorial board was quick to call for federal intervention, disregarding the Cherokee political system in which many opposed their government's action and some called for review of the election in which a small minority of the electorate voted.

Few journalists saw what we considered a balanced starting point, as American Indian Policy and Media Initiative Director Ronald D. Smith writes, "Two distinct and mixed disenfranchised groups pitted against each other over one hundred years ago by the federal government that had little interest in either side."

This case wasn't straightforward for fellows of the American Indian Policy and Media Initiative, either.

Lewis and Clark Law School associate professor and Initiative fellow Robert J. Miller wrote, "The citizens of the Cherokee Nation exercised their sovereignty as a people, as a political entity and as a government to determine the limits of Cherokee citizenship. This is no different than how Americans and the United States government have exercised their sovereign and political authority to define and to strictly control American citizenship. America has placed numerous limitations and conditions on U.S. citizenship. For example, naturalized American citizens such as California Governor Arnold Schwarzenegger can never become the president because they were not born in this country."

Steven Newcomb, author, columnist and Initiative fellow, called on the Cherokee Nation as long as it was expelling people to stop blocking the Delaware Nation's efforts to exist again as an independent nation from the Cherokee.

"If the Cherokee Nation is not bound by the Freedmen provisions of the 1866 treaty with the United States," Newcomb wrote, "then on what basis are the Delawares bound by their 1867 agreement with the Cherokee Nation?"

The news media, as Ronald D. Smith reports in "The Cherokee-Freedmen Story: What the Media Saw" lacked the expertise and failed to do the background reporting, which would have enabled them to accurately and fairly cover this situation.

Native Hawaiian Sovereignty

In the "Indigenous Recognition and Self-Governance Morph into 'Race Wars'" Patricia R. Powers presents the kind of summary and abstract that the Friends Committee on National Legislation routinely prepares for members of Congress.

It gives a snapshot of how media and right-wing Congressional leaders converged effectively to put the Native Hawaiian Government "in a class with controversial issues such as flag-burning or gay rights," Powers writes.

The bill would have established a governing body like those of mainland tribal nations for the estimated 400,000 Native Hawaiians. It would be based on their distinct identity, their need for management over land and other resources, and their need for support of the population which is disproportionately poor, sick and incarcerated.

But the opposition that the bill faced leading up to the June 8, 2006 vote was out of proportion with what Hawaiian leaders said was a local legislative fix. As the date approach it grew increasingly clear that the opposition was far better financed than predictable opponents in Hawaii could afford. The *New York Times* editorialized against the misplaced fears of critics who warned that "a Pacific paradise will become balkanized banana republic." Yet Hawaiian leaders remember observing then-Senate Majority Leader Bill Frist on the phone gathering opposition votes.

The bill narrowly failed on a procedural vote that would have brought it to the Senate floor. The bill needed sixty affirmative votes, but got only fifty-six, with forty-one opposed and three absent.

Six months later representatives of the Office of Hawaiian Affairs told close to four hundred tribal officials gathered at the Tribal Leader's Forum in San Diego in January 2007 about how easily the alignment against the Akaka bill could be turned against tribal sovereignty on the mainland.

"You read the bill and you substitute Native American for Native Hawaiian," said Alan Parker, Chippewa Cree and former chief counsel to the U.S. Senate Committee on Indian Affairs, to representatives of the Office of Hawaiian Affairs, "and you realize that your bill wound up being a proxy."

Looking Ahead

"On January 17, 2007—114 years to the day after the illegal overthrow of the Hawaiian kingdom—Senator Daniel Akaka reintroduced a version of the *Native Hawaiian Government Reorganization Act of 2007*," the Office of Hawaiian Affairs reported on its web site. The bill, the office explains, has a stronger potential because of the inclusion of some revisions made after consulting the Bush Administration two years ago.

At the Tribal Leader's Forum a couple of weeks earlier in January a speech by Hawaii's senior Senator Daniel K. Inouye was read because he was unable to attend. Yet as Patricia Zell, Navajo and Arapaho and another former chief counsel of the Senate Committee on Indian Affairs, read the warning, "be sure you do nothing that in the public eye would make you seem dispensable," it was as though the Senator himself was present:

> I hope that if you haven't had the opportunity to do so, you'll take a few moments and acquaint yourselves with some of the words spoken by various members of the Senate when the Native Hawaiian recognition bill came to the floor of the Senate. Rest assured, those Senators were not talking about conditions in the State of Hawaii, they were talking about Indian country when they spoke of the dire consequences that would flow from the recognition of another Native government. When

they spoke of race-based governments, they were talking about tribal governments. When they talked about racially-defined enclaves, they were talking about Indian reservations. When they warned members that State jurisdiction would be rolled back and local governments would lose millions in taxes, they were talking about Indian country. That debate should speak volumes to you about the political climate in the Senate when it comes to matters of Native sovereignty.

Following the Cherokee vote in March, Bruce Fein, the *Washington Times* opinion columnist, constitutional lawyer and conservative activist, demonstrated how closely linked issues such as the Cherokee Freedmen situation, the Native Hawaiian legislation and tribal sovereignty are in the hands of those who would cleverly appropriate civil rights ideals, making themselves appear to be enlightened as they turn to harm indigenous America.

In this column, published by the *Washington Times* on March 6, Fein calls on Congress to "prohibit racial discrimination by Indian tribes, reject a Native Hawaiian government ... and make colorblindness the soaring signature of the United States in all its laws and policies."

Colorblindness is an offensive white suggestion in a nation, like the United States, which was built on the backs of so-called racial minorities and on Native nations' lands.

It is unseemly how convenient it is for the racial elite of the U.S., who once used our skin colors and other aspects of our appearance against us, to say now that our beauty is celebrated, our arts popular and our economic and political influence growing that the U.S. should all of a sudden become colorblind.

Whenever this idea surfaces, be quick to call it what it is: the twenty-first century adaptation of racism.

▼ ▼ ▼   —Kara Briggs, Editor

The Cherokee-Freedmen Story: What the Media Saw

– By Ronald D. Smith –

National media and U.S.-based international journalists were watching in Oklahoma on the first weekend in March 2007, as voters in the Cherokee Nation decided issues of citizenship. The news reporters looked at the same situation and often talked with the same people. But they didn't always see the same story.

Some journalists saw the Cherokee-Freedmen story as one about civil rights of African Americans, an issue of race, rights and justice. Some saw it as being about Cherokee sovereignty or about Indian identity and how that is determined.

Few saw it as the case of two distinct and mixed disenfranchised groups pitted against each other one hundred years ago by the federal government that had little interest in either side, a struggle that is still being played out today.

Fewer still saw it as a complicated story rooted in the importance of lineage within a wider society in which lineage does not have the political weight it does in Native America.

Research Methodology

This research is an analysis of coverage of a news event that focused on the historical and contemporary relationship between one tribal nation and a closely related group of African Americans, generally as told through the eyes of the mainstream media. This focus is important because it is through mainstream media that most Americans get their information about Indians, unlike other issues in which people may have more direct personal experience.

The research questions included:

- How did mainstream news media present their coverage of the Cherokee-Freedmen story? Particularly, how did they deal with sometimes competing issues such as the governmental sovereignty of the Cherokee Nation and the status and rights of the Freedmen?
- What news sources did the mainstream media rely on in their coverage of the story? Specifically, what was the balance between sources on either side of the issue?

The research involves a content analysis of twenty-six general news reports, including print reports from a seven-day period (March 1–8, 2007) and broadcast transcripts for an eleven-day period (February 27–March 10, 2007). The artifacts examined were headlines and full text of news articles retrieved through online databases from newspapers, broadcast news and wire services. Excluded from the statistical analysis of the articles, but held for later comparison and analysis, are two categories of media reports: opinion (editorials, commentaries, online columns and blogs) and ethnic media (Indian newspapers and black publications).

The content analysis addressed several aspects of the reporting:

- Headlines, and their linguistic hook to attract readers
- Leads, and the information they highlighted
- Quoted news sources, particularly their affiliation and vested interest in the story
- Statistical information about the vote, including raw numbers, percentages, and number of voters
- Use of "racist" and associated/derivative terms
- Use of "sovereign" and associated/derivative terms
- Presentation of a historical context for the story, including information about slavery, treaties and the Dawes Rolls
- Presentation of information about money, gaming, benefits and other financial aspects of the story

The content analysis was conducted March 10–15, 2007, by Ronald D. Smith, communication professor at Buffalo State College and director of the American Indian Policy and Media Initiative based there.

Theoretical Base

Three concepts from communication theory underlie this research: agenda-setting, priming and framing.

The *agenda-setting* theory argues that the mass media, while perhaps not effective in determining how audiences will accept the opinions and point of view in media reports, will nevertheless determine what audiences see as newsworthy. In layman's terms, agenda-setting means that the media may not be able to tell us what to think, but they can tell us what to think about. By the issues they choose to cover and the way those issues are framed, the news media can legitimize a story or some aspect of that story. Conversely, the reporting style also can marginalize aspects of a story. The relevant question within the Cherokee-Freedmen story is how the media placed issues such as racism, sovereignty and historical context on the audiences' agenda.

A related theoretical concept is *priming*. This deals with context. The observation is that the amount of time and space that media devote to an issue make an audience receptive and perhaps alert the audience to particular themes. For example, prior coverage of civil rights, particularly denial of voting rights, may have prepared audiences to see the Cherokee-Freedmen story in that light. Likewise, the story-telling is impacted by the historical context that is known to journalists and audiences alike.

Whereas agenda-setting deals with the perceived newsworthiness of an issue, *framing* focuses on the presentation of the story. How do the news media frame a story? Is there an inherent "good guy" in the story? Whose version of the story gets top billing? Which version becomes the standard against which other points of view are measured? Framing provides for a rhetorical analysis of the text, in this case news reports, to identify perception and/or presentation.

Framing has been called an exercise in power and persuasion. It involves the use of metaphor, spin, story-telling, jargon, word choice, and other narrative elements. The relevant issue to the Cherokee-Freedmen story is the context in which the media reports placed various elements. These include the mixed-race Cherokee community and the convoluted history of both the Cherokee Indians and the

Freedmen. The Freedmen group itself is a mixed group that includes people with Cherokee lineage, other Indian lineage, black lineage and white lineage, of descendants of slaves once held by the Cherokee as well as descendants of black slaves held by others.

Background

Cherokee Nation, with 260,000 enrolled members, is the second largest Indian tribe in the U.S. When European settlers began to arrive, the Cherokee people resided in the area of the Smoky Mountains and what is now Kentucky, Tennessee, Georgia and the Carolinas. Through contact and intermarriage with the settlers, the Cherokee adopted many white practices and became identified as one of "The Five Civilized Tribes." Among the practices incorporated by wealthy Cherokee was the cultivation of farms, along with the dependence on black slaves.

Congress passed the *Indian Removal Act* in 1830 to move all Indian to the west of the Mississippi. In 1838, the Cherokee, including their black slaves, were relocated to Oklahoma Territory in what came to be known as the Trail of Tears, the forced march of thousands of people.

In 1866, the federal government signed a treaty with the Confederate States of the Cherokee Nation, a name reflecting of the tribe's alignment during the Civil War. The treaty required the tribe to absorb its former slaves who had been freed by tribal decree before the war ended—as well as other blacks living in Indian Territory—as citizens of the Cherokee Nation. In return, Washington recognized the Cherokee as a sovereign nation.

Congress created the Dawes Commission, which from 1899 to 1906 conducted a census that identified Cherokees as either entirely or part Indian or as Freedmen, who may or may not have had any Cherokee lineage.

In 1975, the Cherokee Constitution provided citizenship for Cherokees (as well as Delaware and Shawnee Indians adopted into the tribe) identified on the Dawes Rolls. The provision was interpreted as expelling many descendants of the Freedmen. In March 2006, the Cherokee Nation Supreme Court ruled that the citizenship language in the constitution was too vague to exclude Freedmen and that the nation could vote on the issue. A special election was called to amend the constitution to limit citizenship to those who are "Cherokee by blood" (descendants of those whom the Dawes Commission had identified as Indian) and rescinded citizenship for those descended solely from persons whom the commission listed as Intermarried Whites or as Freedmen.

Opponents of the proposed amendment appealed to federal court, and in February 2007 a federal judge in Washington ruled that the amendment vote could continue. At that time, about 2,700 Freedmen were on the tribal rolls, with estimates of 42,000 non-enrolled descendants of the original Freedmen.

The vote was held March 3, 2007. Turnout among the nation's 45,000 registered voters was higher than usual for tribal elections, with 8,743 votes cast: 6,702 to accept the amendment (76.8%), 2,041 (23.3%) to reject it.

Media Coverage

The scope of this study is how the news media reported on the March 3, vote. The vote was widely covered by mainstream media, including newspapers, wire services and broadcast media. The Associated Press had frequent updates on the day of the vote, reporting the adjustments in the tally as the votes were reported. Wire services sent the story around the world.

Headlines

Headlines in articles prior to the vote tended to be neutral: "Cherokee Tribe Faces Decision on Freedmen" *(Morning Edition, NPR)*, "Putting to a Vote the Question 'Who Is Cherokee?'" *(New York Times)*, "Cherokees to Vote: Can Freedmen Be Native American?" *(Voice of America News)*, "Cherokees to Vote on Bloodlines" *(Washington Times)*.

After the vote, some of the headlines remained neutral: "Cherokees Vote to Cut Members" *(Albany Times Union)*, "Cherokee Vote on Membership Issue" *(Birmingham News)*.

Some reported the outcome of the vote in factual, non-emotional terms: "Slave Descendants Lose Tribal Status" *(New York Times)*, "Tribe Votes to Remove Freedmen Descendants; Cherokee Nation Limits Membership to Indian Blood" *(Oklahoma City Oklahoman)*.

However, other headlines used language with more emotion-laden content: "Tribe Revokes Freed Slaves' Membership" *(Associated Press Online)*, "Cherokee Vote Revokes Membership of 2,800" *(Cleveland Plain Dealer)*, "Slave Descendants Ousted by Cherokees" *(Associated Press Online)*, "Cherokee Kick Out Freedmen" *(Tulsa World)*. International media showed a particular penchant for emotion-rich language: "Cherokees Disown Slave Descendants" *(Sydney, Australian)*; "Cherokees Accused of Racism by Black Tribesmen" *(Edinburgh Scotsman)*, "Cherokees Accused of Racist Plot as Sons of Slaves Are Cast Out" *(Times of London)*.

The day-two follow-up stories generally had a future slant: "A Legal Battle: Cherokee Freedmen to Fight for Inclusion" *(ABC News)*, "Cherokee Freedmen to Fight for Inclusion" *(USA Today)*, "What Will Happen to Freedmen?" *(Oklahoman)*, "Future Uncertain for Cherokee's Freedmen Descendants after Vote to Drop Them from Tribe" *(America's Intelligence Wire*, AP Worldstream*)*, "Black Cherokees to Challenge Ouster from Tribe" (Reuters).

Online reports, columns and blogs also addressed the issue with headlines such as "Cherokees Vote Descendants of Slaves Off Tribal Rolls" *(Huffington Post)*, "Someone Is Gonna Be Red in the Face" *(Political Cortex)*, "Resurgent Racism" *(Washington Times* column)*, "Cherokee Voters Say 'Yes' to Self-righteous Racism" *(Meadville KS Tribune* column)*, "Black Cherokees to Fight Ouster From Tribe" *(Monsters and Critics.com)*, "The Cherokee Nation's 'Ethnic Cleaning' Is Not Acceptable" *(ER Shipp blog)*, "A New Twist on the 'One Drop' Rule" *(Just Democracy blog)*, "Cherokee 'Nation' Is Racist: Where's the Outrage?" *(Canadian Sentinel blog)*.

Black media and columnists tended to be direct: "Cherokee Nation Ousts Blacks" *(New America Media)*, "It's All about Money, Political Clout" (column in *Bradenton (FL) Herald)*, "Saying No to Blacks" *(History News Network)*.

Indian media reports were mixed. Some were neutral: "Cherokees Vote to Revoke Membership of Freedmen" *(Indian Country Today)*, "Cherokee Nation Special Election Results" *(Native American Times)*. Some reporting was critical of the Cherokee decision: "Racism and the Cherokee Nation" *(Taino online)*, "Cherokee Nation Ignores Own Treaty" *(Indianz.com* column)*, "Cherokee Nation Takes the Lower Road" *(Indianz.com* column)*, "Ouster of Freedmen a Low Point for Cherokees" *(Indianz.com* editorial)*.

Vote Count

Most of the reports did not give the specific vote count. Fifteen articles (58%) reported that the amendment passed with 77% support. Only five articles (19%) reported the number of votes cast, either for and against or in total. None calculated the percentage of voter turnout.

Despite the fact that the voter turn-out represented less than 3.4% of the Cherokee population and about 19% of the nation's registered voters, this was not considered a newsworthy fact by most media reports. One report noted that turnout was greater than in most elections. None reported that this was the first single-item topic ever on the ballot, and that the lack of candidates or other issues on the ballot may have affected the turn out.

Additionally, none of the article pointed out that enrolled Freedmen were among the registered voters.

News Sources

A review of the twenty-six news reports shows that the most frequently quoted news sources were Chad Smith, principal chief of the Cherokee Nation; Mike Miller, a spokesman for the Cherokee tribe; Marilyn Vann, president of the Descendants of Freedmen of the Five Civilized Tribes, and Jon Velie, attorney for the Freedmen group. Both sides received equal play. Either Smith or Miller was cited in 74% of the reports (Smith in 69% of the reports, Miller in 54%, with 27% of the articles citing both sources). On the other side, Vann was cited in 73% of the reports; her group's attorney was cited in 15% of the reports, all of those in the same articles quoting Vann.

However, they didn't necessarily receive equal billing. One of the issues associated with framing theory is the relative news value of pro versus con sources; that is, supporters of an issue as compared with opponents. Does the telling of the story focus on the antagonist, the protagonist, or both? If the latter, to what balance? A parallel issue in framing theory is the observation that the one who defines the frame by telling the story first often sets the tone to which other voices are set in opposition.

In the Cherokee-Freedmen story, the Cherokee chief or his spokesman was cited first in only three of eighteen articles quoted both sides (17% of the stories quoting sources; 12% of all the reports).

However, the leader of the Freedmen association protesting the amendment was cited first in fifteen of the eighteen articles citing both sides (83% of the stories quoting sources; 58% of all the reports). Thus by five to one, the "out" voice spoke before the "in" voice; the Freedmen viewpoint was presented before the Cherokee government's position.

Additionally, eleven articles (42% of all the reports) cited a Freedman descendant, generally in the contest of personalizing the situation, particularly the person's need for medical and other services. Six articles (23%) cited supportive members of the Cherokee Nation and four articles (15%) cited a single dissenting Cherokee.

A report by *Agence France Presse* quoted only the Cherokee tribal council member who opposed the amendment, which quote attributed to an article in the *New York Times*. The *Times* itself had cited four additional sources, including the tribal spokesman, the president and attorney for the Freedmen group, and another member of the tribal council who supported the amendment.

Racial Theme

The issue of racism loomed large in some reporting. Eighteen articles (69%) specifically used the word "racism," two-third of those in the lead or opening paragraphs.

Local television KOTV gave perspective in its opening statement: "The Freedmen believe it's racism, and the Cherokees say it's simply a matter of blood." CNN, in its third paragraph, noted without examples that "the tribe is defending itself against accusations of racism."

A report published in both Australia and the United Kingdom hit the racism issue hard in the first paragraph: "Cherokees voted yesterday to expel descendants of black slaves they once owned, a move that has exposed the unsavory role played by some Native Americans during the Civil War and renewed accusations of racism against the tribe." The report later said that opponents of the vote "denounced it as a racist plot to deny tribal revenue." This was the report that generated "racism" rhetoric in the headlines.

Several reports quoted a Freedman attorney charging the tribe with racism and also quoted a Cherokee spokesman defending against the racism charge.

Only three reports (12%) used the crucial words "solely" or "mostly" in explaining that people whose lineage is only from the Dawes Roll

Freemen would lose their claim to citizenship, or otherwise noting that descendents of Freedmen who also are descended from persons identified at Indian on the Dawes Rolls would retain their citizenship based on that lineage.

Instead, most reports implied that the vote would rescind citizenship for all Freedmen. Two reports used a statement attributed to the Freedmen president, Marilyn Vann: "There are Freedmen who can prove they have a full-blooded Cherokee grandfather who won't be members. And there are blond people who are 1/1000 Cherokee who are members." What the reports did not address was the context that lineage and enrollment/citizenship are different issues.

Racism & Sovereignty

Racism and sovereignty themes were similar in quantity but not in quality of placement. As noted above, the racism theme figured in 69% of the reports; sixteen articles (62%) referred to self-determination. However, the racism theme was played mainly in the opening paragraphs, but less than a third of reports used the self-determination theme in the top paragraphs.

Additionally, in the sixteen articles mentioning self-determination, most cited "tribal officials" or "supporters." Only four articles (15% of the research sample) cited the Cherokee principal chief. Three of those quoted his statement that "the right of self-government [is] affirmed in twenty-three treaties with Great Britain and the United States."

Few articles dealt directly with the concept of sovereignty. The word "sovereignty" was used by only three reports (12%), none of which defined the term. None of the reports included the important nuance—that American Indian tribal nations assert pre-existing sovereign authority based on their legal autonomy that predates the arrival of European settlers who created the U.S. government. Nor did the reports explain that the determination of citizenship is a function of that sovereignty.

Most international media put the concept of self-determination in context. *Voice of America News* noted in its first paragraph that "American Indian tribes are considered sovereign nations within the United States." *Voice of America* was the only piece to note the juxtaposition of the racism and sovereignty themes, when it cited a Freedman spokesperson that "the 1866 treaty's protection outweighs the tribe's claims to sovereignty on this issue."

Meanwhile, a piece by *Agence France Presse* pointed out in its final of ten paragraphs: "Native American tribes recognized by the United States government have the right to self-determination and authority similar to U.S. states." AFP was the only news medium even to try to explain the significance of tribal sovereignty.

Even the sensationalized report in Australian, British and Scottish media reported that "supporters say it was a long overdue move by Cherokees to determine their own tribal make-up."

Question of Money

A report for the Associated Press, also used by Associated Press *Online*, and a companion story by the same reporter for Associated Press Worldstream each focused on the issue of tribal medical and other benefits. In total, twelve articles (46 percent) focused on the issue of tribal money and benefits as a contributing factor in the strained relationship between the Cherokees and the Freedmen. Several implied that the Cherokee vote was caused by desire to eliminate Freedmen claims on tribal money, such as the Australian report that said the decision was made "to block them from claiming a slice of the tribal pie."

Slavery Past

The historical fact that the Cherokees owned African slaves was noted in nineteen articles (73%). Two-thirds of those, twelve articles, reported this in the lead paragraph, five others in the second or third paragraph. Thus 89% of the reports dealing with slave ownership did so in the first three paragraphs. In addition, five articles (19% of the total sample) mentioned rather ambiguously that the Freedmen were descendants of ex-slaves adopted into the tribe.

Dawes Commission

Twelve articles (46% of the sample) specifically mentioned the Treaty of 1866. Most of the reports rooted this in the context of support for the Freedmen, referring to provisions or guarantees in the treaty.

The report to Australian, British and Scottish newspaper, however, noted that the tribe "was essentially forced to sign [the treaty] with the U.S. Government after the Civil War."

Fourteen articles (54%) mentioned the Dawes Committee—six articles (23% of the total sample) mention the Dawes Commission in passing, eight articles (31% in a negative context ("bent on breaking up Indians' collective lands") or as using arbitrary standards ("eyeballed and interviewed those who came before them").

Three articles by the *Washington Post*, the *New York Times* and the Associated Press, explained the workings and results of the commission as an underlying cause of the current controversy. The AP report identified in paragraph 3 the Dawes Commission as follows: "The commission, set up by a Congress bent on breaking up Indians' collective lands and parceling them out to tribal citizens, drew up two rolls, one listing Cherokees by blood and the other listing freedmen, a roll of blacks regardless of whether they had Indian blood."

National Public Radio identified the commission as "a federal government list of Cherokees and members of four other tribes living on Indian lands around 1900. The Dawes Rolls had become the gold standard determining tribal citizenship," not addressing the arbitrary designations that resulted from the commission.

Editorial Comment

The *New York Times* has a pattern of editorializing on the subject of tribal citizenship, all of this precedent falling against the Cherokee action. In April 2002, The *Times* commented on another tribe in a similar situation: "The Seminole Tribe, Running from History: An 'Afro-Indian' Tribes Tries to Bury Its Roots." The editorial was occasioned by the decision to drop black Seminoles from tribal membership. The editorial dug into the Seminole's multi-racial history that, from early on, included a mix of Indians and black slaves. The newspaper's message was clear: "Federal courts will decide whether the Seminoles' treatment of the black brethren is legal. But the court of public opinion will find it mean-spirited and immoral."

In September 2003, the newspaper entered the same arena with another editorial: "When Racial Discrimination Is Not Just Black and White: Race Discrimination Against Black Native Americans." The newspaper said the tribes' sovereignty claim "sounds suspiciously like the 'states' rights' dodge raised by the South when blacks were being murdered for seeking the right to vote." It said the government has placed limits on sovereignty and has laws guaranteeing minority rights.

After the 2007 vote, the *Times* editorialized in a consistent manner. It called the Cherokee vote "a moral low point in modern Cherokee history" and called on the federal government to protect the Freedmen. The newspaper again nodded to the Indian claim of self-determination, adding "but the tribal history makes clear that it is about discrimination—and that it is illegal." The same editorial ran in the *Times*-owned *International Herald*, based in Paris.

To its journalistic credit, the *Times'* editorial stance did not noticeably impact its news reporting. A lengthy article prior to the vote provided a historical perspective on the Freedmen. The first-cited news source was a pro-amendment Cherokee and former deputy tribal chief. Vann of the Freedman association was quoted, with an immediate refuting quote from Miller, the Cherokee Nation spokesman. Later quoted was the attorney for the Freedman group and a Cherokee tribal council member opposed to the amendment.

The *Washington Times*, meanwhile, in an editorial titled "Resurgent Racism" echoed a theme by the Freedman group that the decision would "expel Freedmen with a full-blooded Cherokee grandfather, but [permit] membership to blond people of European ancestry who are 1/1000 Cherokee." The editorial accused a Cherokee advocate of echoing the Ku Klux Klan. It went on rail against the pending *Native Hawaiian Government Reorganization Act*.

A column on "Cherokee Perks" in Slate online focused on the financial aspects of the story. It pointed to free health care, other medical assistance, and scholarships. What the column didn't say is that the "perks" are not limited to the Cherokee and that many of the benefits could be available from the federal government to anyone who can prove tribal lineage, regardless of enrollment.

Black Media

Much of the reporting for specifically African-American audiences occurred in the context of columns and editorials. In general, these have been uniformly against the Cherokee decision. For example, a column in the *Bradenton (FL) Herald*, identified money as the root of the issue, asking: "Doesn't this also have something to do with those billions of dollars the Indian nations reap from gambling?" A column in the *Meadville (Kan.) Tribune* lamented that the Cherokee, once "forced from their land, denied civil rights and treated as worthless dregs, unfit for life within the new society" were treating the Freedmen in the same manner. "All civilizations are prone to monumental mistakes, but such self-righteous racism and greed disguised as self-determination are traits that should be met with our disgust."

The *Washington Afro American* commentary in *New America Media* featured two black journalists who are linked to the Freedmen. They had initiated an e-mail discussion within the National Association of Black Journalists. The column writer advised them to join the Native American Journalists Association as well.

American Indian Media

The American Indian press had its own takes on the issue, more than one. The *Native American Times* report drew heavily on the Associated Press report.

Indian Country Today also used the AP report as its principal news story about the vote, but that story was posted online several days after initial coverage that included a 950-word commentary by Chad Smith, principal chief of the Cherokee Nation, and an even-longer counter-column by Sheryl Lightfoot, chair of the American Indian Policy Center at St. Paul, Minn. An ICT editorial applauded the lack of federal interference, respecting Cherokee sovereignty, but it criticized the timing of the vote, which drew down media attention focused on the anniversary of the "Bloody Sunday" events in Selma, Ala.

Conclusion

What do we learn from this analysis? Interpretation, like beauty, is in the eye of the beholder, but a few common threads can be observed.

- In general, the Cherokee-Freedmen story was reported as a classic clash between oppressor and victim. Missing were nuance, historical perspective, and a context within which to understand the contemporary significance of the story.
- Spokespeople on both sides of the issue had their say in

the news reporting, and but opponents of the amendment (Freedmen president Marilyn Vann and attorney Jon Velie) generally were quoted before Cherokee officials (Principal Chief Chad Smith and spokesman Mike Miller).

- Both issues of racism and self-determination were discussed, but the racism theme figured more prominently (that is, sooner) in the story than the self-determination theme.
- Few reports gave details or context to the vote itself, either the voting numbers or the voter turnout.
- Nearly two-third of the reports raised the money/benefits issue, generally without supporting information, as a factor motivating the vote.
- Most of the articles highlighted the slave-owning history of the Cherokees, but few explained the incorporation of former slaves into the tribe, the incorporation of other people's former slaves, or the confusion created by the Dawes Commission.
- Overall, this is another instance of mainstream media failing to understand the complexity of an issue involving American Indians and their oversimplification of a complex situation.

Ronald D. Smith *is professor and chairman of the communication department at Buffalo State College in New York. He is director of the American Indian Policy and Media Initiative. He is the author of four text books and has a professional background in journalism and public relations.*

The Amazonian Navajo Women © 2005 Frank Salcido

Indigenous Recognition and Self-Governance Morph into 'Race Wars'

– By Patricia R. Powers –

Friends Committee on National Legislation abstract:
A qualitative examination of framing and catchphrases, written by a non-Native with an interest in the rhetoric used in promoting or opposing bills that affect Indigenous peoples. This modest overview draws from written sources as diverse as blogs and editorials. The character of the public and congressional debate of the *Native Hawaiian Government Reorganization Act* puts it in a class with controversial issues such as flag-burning or gay rights. For example, the debate increasingly focused on dire predictions of the havoc passage the Akaka bill would wreak on the U.S. Moreover, the decibels and the stridency of the debate tended to cloud the real issues and skew the meaning of proposals that would affect many groups in Hawaii. An attitude towards a whole people was symbolized by opponents' lack of interest in and dismissiveness of Native Hawaiian culture. The most discomforting aspect of the debate over the bill was the emphasis on reverse discrimination and race-based government by vociferous opponents, raising the question: Are there implications for the continuation of tribal sovereignty?

> Unlikely as it seems now, your grandchildren may one day need a passport to sunbathe in Maui.
> —Kathryn Jean Lopez, *National Review Online*

There wouldn't be space in ten columns for a detailed

examination of all the mischief created by the bizarre and antiquated citizenship status of Indians in the United States. Yet, believe it or not, Congress has under serious consideration legislation to create a similar caste problem in Hawaii.

—John Dendahl

This bill has brought out, or has brought to the surface, a lot of what people are uncomfortable with about Indian Country. It's like a wave coming in and turning up the sand at the shore.

—Patricia Zell, *Indian Country Today*

Native Hawaiian Reorganization Act of 2005

While aboriginal people have lived on Hawaii for more than a thousand years, the overthrow of the Kingdom of Hawaii in 1893 and its subsequent annexation by the United States in 1898 without the consent of the Hawaiian people means there is no federally recognized Native governing body. The *Hawaii Admission Act* and the Hawaii constitution recognize the rights of indigenous people. However, entities and offices which now represent 400,000 indigenous Hawaiians do not have government-to-government relationships with the U.S. comparable to those enjoyed by federally recognized Native nations or tribes in the lower forty-eight states and Alaska. A recent legislative effort centered on re-establishing identity, exploring self-governance and more independence.

A seven-year effort by state and federal officials and thousands of indigenous people to obtain federal recognition and some degree of self-government for Native Hawaiians ended in defeat in the U.S. Senate in June 2006. Depending on one's viewpoint, this was a positive or negative development. However, the way it was "killed" was discomforting if not startling to many of us. For example, in the month before the vote, editors of the *Wall Street Journal* grumbled that the recognition-reorganization bill, like movie horror figure "Freddy Krueger," refuses to die (*Wall Street Journal* 2006).

Brief Legislative History

To back up a little, on September 26, 2000, a bill to recognize Native Hawaiians passed the U.S. House of Representatives but never made it on the Senate floor due to opposition that materialized from conservatives in Congress, supported by the *Wall Street Journal* and the *National Review*. Bills had been introduced by the Hawaiian congressional delegation, in part to address recent developments. Supreme Court decisions threatened to undermine current programs of value to Native Hawaiians. They triggered a need for Congress to clarify the political status of Native Hawaiians.

One court case necessitated a rethinking of how to create some type of entity to represent their interests because the Office of Hawaiian Affairs, part of state government, had also been challenged in the courts. This case was brought by U.S. Solicitor General Theodore Olsen. The state of Hawaii hired John Roberts, now Chief Justice of the Supreme Court, to defend the right of the Hawaiian affairs office to have its board made up entirely of Native Hawaiians. Roberts lost the case because Native Hawaiians were considered a racial category rather than a group with unique political status.

The Native Hawaiian recognition bills were supported by the governor and attorney general and by Hawaii's U.S. senators and representatives, as well as by American Indian and Native Alaskan organizations and the Leadership Conference on Civil Rights. Support also came from the National Council of La Raza, the Japanese American Citizens League, the Organization of Chinese Americans, the National Asian Pacific American Legal Consortium, and others. While many publications such as *Indian Country Today* supported the effort, other Native news outlets opposed it because they did not believe the bills were in the best interest of the original people in Hawaii.

The proposed legislation was not a simple fix. Questions arose in Congress about how to define a Native Hawaiian, what to do about those with some blood lineage who had moved away from the island, whether changes would introduce casinos into Hawaii which does not allow gambling, and other topics. Some were red herrings and some arose out of genuine concern.

Brief Political History

At the start of the 109th Congress in 2005, bills S. 147 [later S. 3064] and H.R. 309 were still treated as fairly routine. After all, many states work to fix their problems with federal legislation and their elected officials explain to their fellow senators and representatives the importance of the proposed law. The resulting bills are tinkered with but generally pass. However, Secretary of Interior Gale Norton criticized the bill. Then Senator Daniel Kanihina Akaka (D. Hawaii) had to meet objections of the Bush administration's Justice Department about federal liability, military readiness, civil and criminal jurisdiction and gaming, but he stated that the compromises did not hurt the basic intent of the bill. One Native source of information noted: "Conservative Republicans and organizations have been heavily lobbying the Senate to oppose the measure. Through newspaper columns, web sites, public forums and other methods, they argue that Congress doesn't have the power to create a 'race-base' government" (*Indianz.com* 2005).

Initially, the Akaka bill—named after its sponsor—had bipartisan support. Republican Governor Linda Lingle, who was adamantly in favor of the bill, won the support of a number of Republicans. Then the political climate began to change. The *Washington Times* newspaper continued to oppose the proposed legislation and in June 2005, the Senate Republican Policy Committee opposed the bill. The proposed legislation became controversial. It was viewed with alarm by a certain non-native, non-Hawaiian, conservative faction which created "a swell of opposition" (Brisco, 2005). Increasingly the objections and rhetoric focused on race while the bill was about the political status of Indigenous people. President Bush's administration moved from concerned but neutral to outright opposition. Despite months of negotiation and compromises to accommodate administration objections, a letter in opposition was sent by the administration less than twenty-four hours before the key Senate vote on June 8, 2006. Supporters lost the vote.

The vote was very close, in part because Senator Daniel Inouye (D.-Hawaii) had worked for several years to line up his colleagues and get their commitments. Apparently, he also worked out some vote trading with other senators. He secured a promise from the Senate Majority Leader to get a vote on the floor. Perhaps the bill would have passed had it been voted on when originally scheduled but the aftermath of destructive Hurricane Katrina postponed the vote for months. Three senators did not vote; forty-two Democrats and thirteen Republicans voted to let the Akaka bill move on, and forty-one Republicans voted to stop its progress. The fifty-six to forty-one vote fell short of the sixty votes needed to free the stalled bill.

Following the Akaka Bill

I provide the information above to orient readers unfamiliar with Native Hawaiian recognition and reorganization efforts. Appendix A provides a brief legislative history. However, my article is NOT: (1) a detailed explanation of the Senate bill sponsored by Senator Akaka or its companion bill in the House; (2) reasons why different groups of Native Hawaiians supported and opposed these bills; (3) the usual procedural maneuvering on Capitol Hill or every nuance of why one version passed in the House in 2000 only to have the Senate version fail in 2006; or (4) an endorsement of the *Native Hawaiian Reorganization Act of 2005*. The genesis of the article came from an attempt by Quakers to gain a deeper understanding of why some groups of Native Hawaiians supported the bill while other groups strongly opposed it.

Public discussion is a welcome aspect of the passage of any legislation and media blitzes to inspire members of the public to act are routine practice. In the process of monitoring the bill's progress and stalls in Congress, my awareness grew of opposition from well-known people who were not Native Hawaiians or even residing in the state and from well-known conservative commentators and publications. For example, the *National Review* selected the Native Hawaiian "vote to pave the way for secession by racial separatists" as its June 1, 2006 cover story; the word "Shame" looms large on the cover. There was nothing amiss or unethical, but the messages from so many different sources were repetitive and there was an unexpected degree of animus. It is disappointing when any public policy issue diminishes to the level of personal disparagement as was done by some media pundits against Senator Akaka.

Finally, it should be noted that the Akaka bill was opposed by the U. S. Commission on Civil Rights. While that commission is more or less liberal or conservative depending on who sits on it, it has been a moral arbiter at many times so its recommendations are worth reading at its web site (www.usccr.gov). One member of the board from Nevada who voted against the report to oppose the *Native Hawaiian Reorganization Act* is Arlan D. Melendez, chair of the Reno-Sparks Indian Colony, vice president of the Inter-Tribal Council of Nevada, and regional vice president of the National Congress of American Indians. Melendez was appointed to the Commission on Civil Rights by Congress. The concern he voiced at the time of the vote is the same concern that we at the Friends Committee on National Legislation have had. Will those opposed to Akaka decide that it should also be illegal for other Native governments to exist as they do for the hundreds of federally recognized tribes on the mainland and in Alaska?

Background: Quakers Informally Monitor Akaka Bill

Over the centuries, members and leaders of the Religious Society of Friends (Quakers) have interacted and partnered with citizens of Native nations and supported indigenous concerns in many countries including Canada and the U.S. Individual Quakers have worked at the national and local level on projects, in spiritual harmony, and with national organizations representing indigenous people. The international grassroots-oriented Quaker organization, the American Friends Service Committee, has long had a Native American Affairs Program. Our separate Quaker lobbying organization, Friends Committee on National Legislation, has lobbied on Capitol Hill with Native representatives on many issues from sacred sites to Indian trust fund reform. Therefore it should come as no surprise that Quakers would be cognizant of matters involving indigenous peoples.

For this reason, the Friends committee was asked by the Office of Hawaiian Affairs to support legislation to provide a process for gaining federal recognition to Native Hawaiians and to create a vehicle for some type of self-governance. This is a bill that Friends committee might have supported after careful review and consideration because it appeared to recognize the cultural and political uniqueness of another group of indigenous people living in the U.S. It seemed parallel to our other concerns such as reform and restitution of federal American Indian trust funds since it would establish that the Federal Government recognizes the right of Native Hawaiians to manage their own land, money and assets, even though how all would transpire was somewhat nebulous.

However, staff at our sister organization the American Friends Service Committee asked those of us at Friends legislative committee not to lobby for or support the bill. American Friends Service Committee had an office in Hawaii and their staff worked closely with Native Hawaiians who were vigorously opposed to the direction the legislation would take because they viewed themselves as part of a sovereign nation that pre-dated the U.S. and statehood. Other Native

Hawaiians also had weighty reasons for opposing the bill. However, since those are not the subject of this paper, they will not be detailed here. As a consequence, Friends legislative committee was *neutral* about the Native Hawaiian recognition and reorganization companion bills in the House and Senate, the latter referred to as the Akaka bill. The Friends committee did prepare a background piece for its web site.

In most cases, the Friends legislative committee forgoes legislative advocacy when a Native nation or a group of indigenous people are split on what is needed and wanted. The National Congress of American Indians also stays away from situations that involve internal policy disputes. However, in this instance, the NCAI leadership came down firmly on the side of Native Hawaiians, passing four resolutions for federal recognition, gave unwavering support over three or more years, and even provided staff of the Office of Hawaiian Affairs with office space in their office. One early criticism of the proposed legislation was that it would take money away from tribes in the forty-eight contiguous states or money from American Indians and Alaska Natives through the Bureau of Indian Affairs. NCAI emphatically stated this claim was inaccurate. To make its position crystal clear, NCAI joined together with Native Hawaiians in active support of the bill.

We often monitor bills of interest even if we are not going to formally support or oppose them. Friends legislative committee was particularly concerned that the arguments prevailing seemed to be anti-sovereignty positions. As early as July 2001, conservative Michelle Malkin began a column in townhall.com by alleging the following:

> Some people will do anything to get their money on federal wampum. Across the country, scam artists claiming to be oppressed "indigenous peoples" have used dubious family histories, altered documents or shady land claims to win government recognition as Indian tribes. Now there's a new group that wants in on all the special rights, free benefits and racial preferences that accompany sovereign tribal status: Native Hawaiians (Malkin 2001).

Bloggers and pundits continued to question basic laws and sovereignty principles. For example, angelfire.com and hyscience.com reprinted the following testimony given by Kenneth R. Conklin March 134, 2006 to the U.S. Commission on Civil Rights.

If the bill passes Congress, a race-based government can be created to protect the wealth and power of some ethnic Hawaiians and to keep federal dollars flowing to Hawai'i... Indian groups throughout America are claiming special rights to race-based control of "sacred places." In Hawai'i, the old pagan religion is being revised and used to support political claims for racial supremacy in land use policy... (Conklin 2006).

Different Religious Groups

Other faith-based groups monitored the Native Hawaiian legislative effort from a conservative perspective. After the vote that defeated the Akaka bill for now, reporter Chad Groening wrote a 2006 article for Agape News that focused on military implications as well as the potential break-up of the Union. While other articles talked of how Native Hawaiian rights would be a precedent for groups such as the Amish, conservative Frank Gaffney's concerns about dominos effects stretch to Islamists in the U.S.:

A military analyst and former officials in the Reagan Defense Department says it's outrageous that the Senate even considered a bill that opponents contend would have allowed the island of Hawaii to create an autonomous, race-based government capable of pulling the state out of the union if it chose... Frank Gaffney of the Center for Security Policy is among those critical of the legislation. He cites what he sees could have been detrimental impacts on the nation as a whole. "The effect could be to enable this new race-based government to decide that it wants to opt out of the fifty states of this union, taking with it not only the wonderful tourist sites of Hawaii but also the strategically critical military facilities," says the Center president.

While intended to give indigenous Hawaiians some of the same powers of self-governance enjoyed by American Indians, Gaffney fears that the legislation instead could have encouraged other groups to push for the same kind of autonomy. "I think it's entirely possible you'd see people coming out of the woodwork, saying, 'You know that deal that the native Hawaiians got in S-147? We want that, too. We want to be able to govern ourselves in our own way. And if it involves leaving the Union, so be it,'" he suggests. Among those groups pushing for similar powers, he says, would be "...people like the Reconquistas, who think they ought to take back part of the United States for Mexico, or Islamists who think they ought to have the right to run their community by a Taliban-style sharia religious code." Such legislation, he says, also could accelerate the process of unraveling the United States as a nation. "You know, we fought a civil war to keep people from doing this sort of thing," says Gaffney... (Groening 2006).

To reiterate, as the director of the Native American program at Friends Committee on National Legislation, I am writing as an observer of the legislative, political, and mass communications process and not in support of the Akaka bill. Friends legislative committee did sent a letter of concern to all senators about the tenor of the debate by the time the vote came near.

Heritage Foundation Monitors the Akaka Bill

Based on recent Supreme Court decisions, the Heritage Foundation took the position that the *Native Hawaiian Reorganization Act* was unconstitutional and focused attention on the implications of going forward with the Akaka bill. In August 2005, Heritage invited three people to speak:

- Rubellite Kawena Kinney Johnson, emeritus professor, Department of Hawaiian and Indo-Pacific Languages at the University of Hawaii;
- Larry Arnn, president of Hillsdale College and a member of the Heritage board of trustees; and
- John Fund, editorial board member of the *Wall Street Journal* and contributing analyst to Fox News and CNBC.

In May, 2006, the foundation invited these people to speak at their Heritage Lecture: U. S. Senator Lamar Alexander (R-TN) and Ramesh Ponnuru, senior editor of the *National Review*. Host of the lecture Todd Gaziano, director of Heritage's Center for Legal and Judicial Studies, had written articles with others such as Ed Meese, former Attorney General under Ronald Reagan, opposing the Akaka bill. To suggest his caring for all Hawaiian citizens, Gaziano said that he was wearing a shell lei until the Akaka bill "was killed." Senator Alexander, who said the Republicans were split about the Akaka bill, viewed the Native Hawaiian issue as part of a trend that he has been attempting to reverse with bills such as English as the national language.

Regular Opponent Monitors the Bill

Does it sound far-fetched, or a little paranoid, to worry that the highly organized campaign against Native Hawaiian recognition and rights will spill-over to long established Indian tribes? If so, then read: (a) the paragraph below, excerpted from a column written by a leader of a group organized against Native American rights called Citizens Equal Rights Alliance; (b) the self-identification of this critic of the Akaka bill; and (c) the same writer's letter of opposition, titles "Hawaii in Peril."

> Imagine a United States of a mere 50 states, perhaps soon diminished to 49 states. Imagine a United States containing 561 federally recognized Indian tribes operating outside of the U.S. Constitution, along with 274 new Indian "tribes" pursuing a separate, race-based "extra-constitutional" government. Then imagine a separate Hawaiian race-based government, that spawns separate Mexican government homelands and governing "entities" within seven more of our United States (Willman 2006).

Ms. Willman is national chair of the Citizens Equal Rights Alliance and author of a book that chronicles her travels from the East Coast to the West Coast and documents murders, oppression, homeland security concerns and political corruption that stems from our nation's federal Indian policies. She writes the following:

> I'm hoping that you might be willing to write a brief note to your senators and congressmen, opposing the pillaging and plundering of the great state of Hawaii. Should this legislation pass, Barb Lindsay tells us, that you can look for activists to "take back California"—and New Mexico…

and on and on. This dismantling of America through tribalism, MUST come to a screeching halt. The "enrolled" population of a "Hawaii tribe" would nearly DOUBLE the population of enrolled tribal members across the country... giving even more power to the Indian industry, Indian gambling industry and god-knows-what's next... I know Hawaiians thank you and we do too!

Out of his belief that reservations are run by an unconstitutional, un-republican form of government, Howard Hanson, the former chair of the Citizens Equal Rights Alliance wrote a press release about the Akaka bill. It was published in the Resource Sentinel in Minnesota several days before the vote and picked up and carried by the PR Newswire (United Business Media):

> Jack Abramoff may be out of the picture but his corrupt legacy continues as the Senate nears a showdown on the Hawaiian Bill SB 3064 this week... We strongly urge Senators to come to Minnesota and tour the Red Lake, Leech Lake, White Earth, Prior Lake and Mille Lac reservation areas before voting on the bill. We would like for them to see for themselves the ramifications of Tribalism and Treaty Rights and how it economically degrades an area and creates continuous racial conflict while destroying the lives of our Indian friends. (PR Newswire 2006).

The Citizens Equal Rights Alliance is one of several organizations, such as One Nation United (which has 300,000 members), that seek reform of what their members view as a flawed federal Indian policy. A combination of anti-sovereignty, business, industry and agricultural organizations sometimes joins forces. They seek to weaken constitutional protections for Native Americans while stating they are for a free-market economy, level playing fields and fairness. They claim they fight for small-town America, landowners whose rights are abused, non-Indian landowners on Indian reservations, trade groups hurt by Indian competitors, and people opposed to gambling. Such organizations hold annual conferences and have filed friend-of-the-court briefs in Supreme Court cases. They use controversies such as hunting and fishing disputes as a recruitment tool. It may be significant, in terms of the mainland, for a group such as Citizens Equal Rights Alliance to chime in on the Native Hawaiian legislation.

The point is not to valorize supporters of the bill and denigrate opponents. The point is to show how many interest groups became involved and how they repeated each other's phrases and sound bites.

Content Analysis Patterns

A number of individuals and groups in Hawaii have opposed the legislation written and lobbied for by the congressional delegation and Governor. I did not analyze campaigns by these grassroots opponents who had a different vision or had particular objections to aspects of the proposed legislation. Instead, my interest was in those who held that this decision had consequences for the entire country. By way of comparison, congressional leaders will sometimes use their appropriations power to oppose or promote programs or rights for people living in the District of Columbia. They do this to test ideas and implement ideologies that they believe would be helpful throughout the U.S. In many other ways, certain issues become a barometer to measure mood or commitment or values.

Because all national Native organizations had bonded together to support the Akaka legislation, those who discounted this solidarity were of interest to me. Of even more interest were those who took this opportunity to question Native rights and Native sovereignty. To my knowledge, none of the conservative critics of the Akaka bill were from Hawaii, so their opposition flowed from abstract principles; as is sometimes said, they did not have a dog in the race.

As so often happens with the internet today, this low profile legislation became high profile through blogs. One blogger, who analyzed those who opposed the bill for different reasons, entitled the write-up "A Blogospheric Eruption over Hawaii's Future." He gave credit to Michelle Malkin as the individual who most successfully kept the issue before her likely conservative allies who would ultimately pressure Congress to defeat or block the bill.

Opposition to the Native Hawaiian Government Reorganization Act

Partial list of political pundits and leaders who opposed bill
Tucker Carlson

Linda Chavez
Bruce Fein
John Fund
Frank Gaffney, Jr.
Slate Gordon
Rush Limbaugh
Rich Lowry
Michelle Malkin
Ed Meese
Robert Novak
Phyllis Schafly
Paul Weyrich

Partial list of bloggers and web sites that opposed bill
Akakatalka
Aloha 4 all
Angel Fire (Kenneth Conklin)
Betsy's Page
Human Events Online
Point of Law
Political Review (T. Clarkson makes some good points)
Redstate
Townhall

Partial list of newspapers/journals that opposed bill or ran columns
National Review (cover story)
Wall Street Journal (editorials and columns)
Washington Times

Partial list of organizations that opposed bill
Eagle Forum
Heritage Foundation
National Center for Public Policy Research
Property Rights Foundation of America

Key phrases of critique against bill (many repeated dozens of times)
allegedly poor, downtrodden "indigenous" people; balkanize; backdoor to casino gambling; dangerous to all states; hostility toward United States; largest tribe in America; new tribe; outrageous

1993 Hawaiian apology bill; separatist enclaves; special treatment; stealth strategy; race-based government; racial preference; racial separatism; racial spoils system; racism against those with no Hawaiian blood; radicals; reverse discrimination; un-American; unconstitutional.

Titles of some articles
"A Race-based Drift?"
"A Race to Racism: Ascribe It to Tribe"
"Aloha Apartheid"
"The Pineapple Time Bomb"

Statements of proponents of the Akaka bill in documents, news articles, editorials, and on blogs could be analyzed and they too would show patterns of arguments and particular choices of words. Perhaps someone else will do content analysis with that approach. Here, I will give just one example of the rhetoric and reasoning used. Former Senate staffer Patricia Zell wrote an article about the constitutionality of the Akaka bill for the Office of Hawaiian Affairs. In it, she argued against the idea of racial and ethnic divisions. She pointed out that Hawaii's constitution was amended in 1978 to, in her words, "strengthen the fabric of the multi-cultural society that is Hawaii, by honoring the legacy of the aboriginal, indigenous, native people of Hawaii whose culture, history, language and traditions have, for generations, been so enthusiastically embraced by all of the citizens of Hawaii." (Zell 2005).

Conclusion: International Indigenous Effort

I will conclude by quoting from an article in the Hawaii Reporter by John Dendahl, who describes himself as a lifelong New Mexican and a member of the Grassroots Institute of Hawaii Advisory Board. (In June 2006, Dendahl became the Republican candidate for governor of New Mexico).In the article, Dendahl makes it clear that he is concerned about the special status of Navajos and the religious claims of Indians on the mainland even though he is opposed to the Akaka bill:

> This legislation panders to a small, narrow interest to create yet another citizen group with special status. The dismal model

for the Hawaiian bill is the special status of American Indians. Rather than move backward with the Hawaiian bill, Congress should engage serious discussion leading toward normalizing citizenship for Indians. One hears from those wanting to go the opposite way that other countries and the United Nations are considering special status for "indigenous" populations. This isn't Latin America and it isn't the United Nations. This is the United States... (Dendahl 2006).

There was an irony to the timing of this Akaka vote and especially the brouhaha over the spreading of the rights menace. The debate on the Hill was happening concurrently with progress on indigenous rights through the United Nations. In June 2006, the United Nations Human Rights Council adopted the *Declaration on the Rights of Indigenous Peoples*, which now goes to the U.N. General Assembly for ratification. The statement, which has been negotiated over many years, was approved in a role call vote; it has forty-five articles. Significantly, the Indigenous Declaration outlined numerous rights from language, culture, education and health to self-determination and lands, territories and natural resources.

While the Declaration is not binding to governments, it is a positive step, which puts pressure on governments to live up to the objectives of the Declaration and will help improve the lives of millions of Indigenous Peoples, particularly in developing countries. Les Malezer of the Foundation for Aboriginal and Islanders Research Action said, "Now we are recognized as Peoples with the right to self-determination. At last we can work in true partnership with governments to ensure our rights and interests are protected in a true democratic manner" (Deer 2006).

Patricia Powers is legislative secretary on Native American issues for the Friends Committee on National Legislation. She is a PhD in American cultural studies, with specializations in ethnology, social change and media. She is co-author of "Community Practice," a text book published by Oxford University Press.

References

Brisco, D. 2005, Sept. 27. "New Version of Native Hawaiian Bill Announced," *Indian Country Today.*

Conklin, K. 2006. "Protecting Civil Rights in Hawaii," Angelfire.com. Accessed.

Deer, K. 2006, July 2. "UN Rights Council Adopts Indigenous Declaration: Canada Votes Against," *First Perspective National Aboriginal News,* Firstperspective.ca Accessed.

Dendahl, J. 2006, April 9. "Does 'Native' Now Mean 'Balkanize' in America?" *Hawaii Reporter.*

Groening, C. 2006, June 12. "Senate Republicans Foil Attempt to Establish 'Native Hawaiian' Gov't," Agape News.

Indianz.com. 2005, Sept. 28. "Bush Questions Legality of Native Hawaiian Bill" (unattributed). Accessed.

Malkin, M. 2001, July 30. "Apartheid for Native Hawaiians," Townhall.com. Accessed,

PR Newswire. 2006, June 6. "Tribalism is Not Working in Minnesota" (unattributed).

Wall Street Journal. 2006, June 2. "Native Hawaiian Recognition an Ugly Act" (editorial).

Willman, E. D. 2006, May 30. "New Version of the Akaka Bill Released," *Hawaii Reporter.* Posted online July 7, 2006, as "Senate to vote on dismantling America, HumanEvents.com. Accessed.

Zell, P. 2005, Aug. 14. "Roots of Freedom," *Honolulu Star-Bulletin.*

Speech to January, 2007 Tribal Leaders' Forum

—A Speech By Senator Daniel K. Inouye—

*Read at the Tribal Leaders Forum
at the Sycuan Band of Kumeyaay Indians-Owned U.S. Grant Hotel
in San Diego, Ca., on January 8, 2007*

While there are forecasts of dramatic change, as the members of the Senate and House of Representatives begin their work in the 110th session of the Congress, there is much that will remain the same.

For instance, in the Senate, we are a thin majority—fifty-one members who are classified as Democrats, and forty-nine who identify themselves as Republicans. In order to accomplish anything, it is clear that Republicans and Democrats will have to work together.

Many have suggested that the outcome of the 2006 mid-term elections was a mandate from America's voting citizens—a message to members of Congress that partisan ways of doing business has resulted in legislative gridlock—and that the voters want a change in the way the Congress has been conducting business.

I, for one, welcome this change, if we can bring it about.

I entered the Congress many decades ago at a time when the more senior members of Congress actually took those of us who were new to the body under their wings and taught us how to get things done.

And one of the first things they told us was that "there is always a tomorrow."

I have relied on that sage advice hundreds of times over the course of the last forty-plus-years, and as a result some of my very best friends in the Senate can be found on the other side of the aisle.

It is well known that the senior Senator from Alaska, Ted Stevens, is my best friend in the Senate. We refer to one another as "brothers," and like brothers, sometimes we disagree, but we also know that there will always be a tomorrow, as well as another set of issues, and another opportunity to find common ground.

So we occasionally agree to disagree with the understanding that we need to cooperate and collaborate more often than we will find ourselves at odds on any issue.

There is a bit more of a disparity in the ratio of Democrats to Republicans in the House, and from time to time, we seem to see deeper divides amongst members there.

However, I would suggest that it is in no one's interest to try to take advantage of those divides, because the lines are drawn differently on almost every issue.

In the game of politics, your friends are your friends and your opponents must be your friends as well.

That is what I mean when I suggest that "there is always a tomorrow."

Native America has become a rather sophisticated old hand at educating members of Congress, especially the new members of Congress, about your challenges and your concerns.

Once again, as you have at the beginning of every new Congress, you will be wanting to spend some time not only with those who represent you directly, but with those members and their staffs who hold key positions on committees of jurisdiction over Native matters.

This year, we begin the Congress with the need to address the unfinished business from the last session of the Congress; The reauthorization of the *Indian Health Care Improvement Act* and trust fund management reform are amongst the highest priorities of the new Chairman of the Senate Indian Affairs Committee, Senator Byron Dorgan.

I believe that many of use who serve your interests in the Congress also place a high value on stimulating economic growth in Native communities.

We understand that while gaming has been a successful field of endeavor for some tribes, gaming has not proven to be an economic panacea for all in Indian country.

And amongst those Native nations that have experienced success in the gaming arena, many acknowledge that gaming is not going to be around forever, and that there is a need to diversify and become less reliant on gaming as a source of economic development.

Some have turned to government contracting—and some have been very successful—so successful that you now have a new set of detractors to contend with.

When you encounter these kinds of negative reactions to your success, you have to wonder whether those who seem to want to bring you down are effectively saying that the American dream is for some but not for all. At least not for you.

This is not a new phenomena. The grand old leaders of Indian Country encountered the same thing in their times but they forged ahead with their mission always in the forefront of their minds.

They were determined and they achieved their goals. So will you.

But in these times, and as your friend, I would inject a note of caution.

As we have seen consistently over the ages, there have been and likely always will be, those who seek to divide you.

If your nations and governments are divided, those who seek your demise won't have much work to do.

If they see that you are willing to throw one another off the side of the ship of state, they will rub their hands together in pleasure and do everything they can to assist you in that regard.

I respectfully suggest, don't do that to one another and don't engage in actions that suggest to the public eye that is always watching you, that one or more of your nations and governments are dispensable.

Sooner or later, whether you see it that way or not, you'll find that as Native people you were always in the same boat, and that if that boat goes down, you all go down with it.

We don't hear too much discussion of Native sovereignty these days in the Congress. It as almost become a negative image.

I hope that if you haven't had the opportunity to do so, you'll take a few moments and acquaint yourselves with some of the words spoken by various members of the Senate when the Native Hawaiian recognition bill came to the floor of the Senate.

Rest assured, those Senators were not talking about conditions in the State of Hawaii, they were talking about Indian country when they spoke of the dire consequences that would flow from the recognition of another Native government.

When they spoke of race-based governments, they were talking about tribal governments. When they talked about racially-defined enclaves, they were talking about Indian reservations.

When they warned members that State jurisdiction would be rolled back and local governments would lose millions in taxes, they were talking about Indian Country.

That debate should speak volumes to you about the political climate in the Senate when it comes to matters of Native sovereignty.

So we must proceed with those warning signs well in mind.

Like those who came before you, you will not be daunted in realizing your dreams and achieving you goals. But you must be ever mindful that in certain circumstances, those you perceive to be your friends may actually be your enemies.

With that said, I also want to observe that over the last 20 years that you have allowed me to join in the advocacy of your rights and your sovereignty, you have become a powerful political force.

And perhaps sadly, in the same way that your successes are sometimes met with opposition and jealousy. Your prowess in the field of politics has been met with the sensational distortions that characterized the Abramoff scandal.

Don't let that discourage you. See it for what it is and continue to move forward.

You have strong allies in the Congress—and maybe you have just as many faint-hearted so-called friends. But working with your allies and working with one another, you will succeed in carrying on the strong traditions of your ancestors with integrity and honesty and courage.

I have come to know you and I am very, very proud to be your friend.

Senator Daniel K. Inouye is the third most senior member of the U.S. Senate, and recipient of the Medal of Honor for his military service during World War II. He has served as a member of numerous Senate committees, chairing the Defense Appropriations Subcommittee, the Commerce, Justice and Science Subcommittee and the Indian Affairs Committee.

Tribute To John C. Mohawk

The late John C. Mohawk gave the following speech at "Hear Our Story: Communications and Contemporary Native Americans," a conference cosponsored by the American Friends Service Committee and the American Indian Policy and Media Initiative in March 2006. Conference participants included tribal leaders, members of Congress, journalists and scholars. In this, the closing keynote of the conference, John dramatically shifted the focus of conference goers from discussions about high powered media and those who work with it or through it to something more real. And there is nothing more real or powerful than how we survive, and how we pass down stories, stories of survival so that another generation can survive.

John Mohawk was also one of the Initiative's early supporters and first fellows.

Sadly, he died as this book was being prepared for publication.

In a December 15, 2006, obituary in *Indian Country Today*, his long-time collaborator and friend José Barreiro wrote,

> Intensely steeped in the spiritual ceremonial traditions of the Haudenosaunee people through his foundational longhouse culture at the Cattaraugus Reservation in Western New York, Mohawk was one of those rare American Indian individuals who comfortably stepped out into the Western academic and journalistic arenas. He was an enthusiastic participant in this own traditional ways, a legendary singer and knowledgeable elder of the most profound ceremonial cycles of the Haudenosaunee. As a scholar, he represented the Native traditional school of thought in a way that was as authentic as it was brilliantly modern and universal.

Reclaiming Traditional Knowledge for Our Futures

– By John C. Mohawk –

Haudenosaunee scholar and author speaking at "Hear Our Stories: Communication and Contemporary Native Americans," a conference in Washington, D.C. in March 2006

I thought I would begin by talking a little bit about two stories that I heard having to do with the 2004 tsunami. The first one, which was widely reported, said that on one of the islands off the coast of India there is an indigenous people. On the day of the event, a fellow was going down to the beach and he noticed that the water was receding, and receding, and receding far out away from where it usually comes.

He had heard stories passed down from generations before that said when this happens it's time to get away from the shore. So he went back up and he set an alarm. There's this detail that he himself reported in the press. One of the people he went to was his grown daughter.

He said, "We've got to get everybody up the hill away from the water." She said, "Are you drunk?" He said, "No. The water has receded, and, it's in the stories our tribe tells that when this happens the water is going to come back."

So they listened to him and ran for their lives up the hill. And it turned out no one died on that island because they listened, you could say, to the voices of their ancestors.

Another story that was told that I thought was kind of cute.

On another island, the people were by the beach bathing when all of a sudden, they noticed that the elephants had turned around and run away up the hill in a panic. The people thought that's strange elephant behavior. But we'd better do that too. So they followed the elephants up the hill, and, once again, on that island hardly anybody got hurt. There, they were following the knowledge of the elephants' ancestors.

Remembering

Consider this: people who were twenty years old in 1929 turn ninety-six this year. Of course, that means that the vast majority of them are already gone. There are few people who were adults in 1929 who are still with us. There are those of us who are here. Some who as adults heard their stories. But as time has gone by, the stories are fading and our memories of what happened in those years.

If we were to pick five events of the twentieth century that shaped its history in the whole world, there's no question that the Great Depression would be one of the five. Most people would also pick the Bolshevik Revolution and World War II. A lot of people would pick the Vietnam War and the fall of the Berlin Wall. But of those, the most interesting one in a way that impacts us today was what happened in 1929.

In 1929, the world economic system collapsed. If you go back and read about it, it collapsed in ways that today we might find unimaginable. We've come to think of ourselves as impervious to that. We don't think it could ever happen again. But then in 1929, they didn't think it could happen either.

The 1929 collapse was helped a little bit by bad ecological events. There was drought in the Midwest. A dustbowl emerged that made life really awful.

What I derive out of that memory is this: Human beings as a society must have some kind of gene in them that they recover from disasters in such a way that they mostly can't remember the disaster. Even as of now, most of us who were far from the tsunami are thinking less about it all the time. Whatever lessons there were to be learned seem to fade away. Already, people are moving back into the area where the tsunami was so devastating, and they're starting to build buildings there. One who would look at history in the broad sense would almost say, actually, that people don't learn much from experience.

Think of Mount Vesuvius, where, of course, geologists will tell you that that's still an active volcano. Some morning it's going to vaporize everybody nearby. But most think it's not going to happen to us. We're going to get through it.

Two Navajo Women © 2006 Frank Salcido

In Indian Country

When the Great Depression happened Indian Country, actually, was insulated against it. What the Great Depression did was destroy a lot of people who had investments, and those who worked in the jobs that those investments created. So it was very devastating to folks who had depended on wage labor and to some people who depended on the value of the markets.

On the other hand, I've heard Indians say this: "We've lived in a permanent depression. We have the same levels of unemployment as they had then and therefore, the Depression doesn't scare me because we've always lived in the Depression."

But if you think that, perhaps, you didn't talk to the people who lived in the real Depression. You didn't talk to them about the fact that there was no insurance net; that when people ran out of money, they ran out of food; that when people ran out of food, they had to go beg in soup kitchens; that people slept under bridges and men were on the road—walking on the railroad tracks; that the country went into not just an economic depression, but a cultural one.

The years 1929, 1930 and 1931 were terrible years for the whole of the United States, and they were tough on the Indians.

There's a kind of sense of stuff—well, you know—that we were a little bit insulated from that because most of our people were on rural Indian reservations and it didn't hit there.

Well, actually there were a lot of our people who were not on rural Indian reservations in 1929. There were a lot of them who had moved into the city and had gotten jobs. When the Depression hit, a lot of them lost their jobs. Many of them found themselves migrating back to the reservations. By 1931, 1932, 1933, people were marching back.

This was also true, by the way, of rural America. A lot of people who had just left rural America since World War I or during or since World War I found themselves unable to pay their rent on their little apartments. But they still had relatives back on the farms so a lot of those people went back and moved on the farms.

The Coming Depression

Now the thing about living on a farm which is different from living in the city is that when you are living on the farm, even if you don't have money, you can often raise food and chop wood and keep yourself warm, and keep yourself alive. When you're in the city, you don't have those options, which is why poverty in the city can be a lot more demeaning than poverty in the country. At any rate, people adopted a strategy of survival of moving into the countryside. The Indians did too. They moved to the country.

Why am I talking about the Depression? Things couldn't be better. There's an optimism in the country among our young people, especially as these are really good times. The good times are rolling. There's an optimism among our young people that is not shared by people who study the world's economic situation and, especially, the United States' economic situation.

There's a general agreement among the world's best economists that there's going to have to be an adjustment. That the United States cannot keep borrowing as much money as they've been borrowing without a strategy to pay it back, and that just buying Chinese goods is not a way to pay it back. We're borrowing Chinese money to buy Chinese goods.

Most economists think that this as an economic strategy isn't a very good one. They expect that there is going to be a contraction in the value of the U.S. dollar.

I don't know if I need to tell you this, but guess who is going to get the first punch? It's going to be people who haven't built a lot of wealth. There are going to be a lot of people—a lot of Indian people—who are going to feel that first punch.

Back to the 1930s. In my part of the country, people used to talk about it. I suspect they still do talk about things, but, when I was growing up, the two big themes were the Depression and World War II. So I heard lots of stories about the Depression, and I heard lots of stories about World War II. I have a feeling I heard stories about the Depression that young people aren't hearing today. It wasn't all bad. This is what they said happened when the people moved back on the reservation, it wasn't too long before it got clear that the jobs that they had in the city weren't going to be restored very quickly. In any case, people on the reservation have a culture of helping one another. It's just the way people are in the rural areas.

So, what happened? People moved back before too long, and people started rebuilding their homes. They did as they others had been doing before. They raised chickens. They planted gardens. They raised hogs.

By the time World War II came, my reservation was fairly prosperous. Not much cash economy. But people had food to eat. They were warm. They were comfortable, and they weren't suffering. It was because they took care of themselves.

Surviving

Now, we would like to think, "Oh, we could do that again." But I want to point something out. We're not the same people that they were then. They grew up doing that, and most of our young people did not grow up doing that. And a lot of people think that moving back into the country and raising food is simple. No it's not. In fact, the reason that it takes generations to establish is that every piece of land has a perfectly good use. And it takes a long time for people to learn that use. People have to pass that knowledge on from generation to the next generation. When you don't do that for two or three generations, you lose that. So, if it were necessary, you'd have to do it all again.

Sometimes, when I've mentioned this, people have said, "Oh, you're advocating that we go back to subsistence living."

Did I say, we should go back to subsistence living? What I'm saying is that in times of crisis, in times of economic distress, our lands, our skills, our heritage, and our cultures have served to help us survive. It's just a reality.

Subsistence doesn't mean you aim for a level of economic existence that's the bare minimum. Subsistence means that the bare minimum is the worst it ever gets. Okay? When you're going this way, you've got this cushion. You stop here. Without subsistence, you keep going until you hit rock bottom, and rock bottom is not good.

Over the years there has been a conversation that has gone on since the Virginia Colony, since the earliest days. The conversation has always gone sort of like this, we are faced with options in our own communities. We've always asked, which is the best option for survival?

So, in some of our communities, the option was that the Americans, the Canadians, the English, the whoever it was, came and they said, you are deficient in the following ways. And they always had a list.

The top of the list was, "Oh, you're not Christian." So, a good percentage of our people said, "Okay, we'll become Christians. That way, we'll survive." But there was always a percentage that said, "Ain't gonna become no Christian, no how." Then you had two factions. And every time you turned around, there was another set of choices. And the new choices about survival strategies always produced new factions.

Indian Country is driven by factions, which were historically created by choices that people made. Shall we go along with the allotment or should we resist the allotment? One group went along. One group resisted. The ones who went along were called by the ones who resisted, sell-outs. The ones who resisted were called by the ones who went along, old-fashioned.

So, we inherit factions of people established in moments of decisions that were made for survival purposes.

Strategies

I want to tell you that we can forgive all those people from a long time ago, no matter which faction we're on or that we inherit, because, most of the time, there was no survival strategy that worked. Most of the time, whether you became a Christian or not—they stole your land. Most of the time—if you took up whatever they told you to take up—they did it anyway.

But that was also then. This is now. And we're not faced with the same kind of deal now that we were faced with then, and we won't be in the future. It will be different.

So, allow me to make a couple of suggestions about what our thinking, our priority might be for the future.

I think that cultures nurture people. When you don't nurture people you don't have culture. In the dominant culture, there's been a statement that runs kind of like this, and it has to do with that Depression. During the Depression, a survival strategy was adopted. It was a survival strategy that was adopted to enable capitalism to survive the possibility of being overwhelmed by communism. The strategy of survival that was adopted was to create social safety nets for people, which include social safety nets in the form of Social Security, social safety nets in the form of Aid to Dependent Children and a whole range of what you called the New Deal programs.

The memory of people sleeping on the street, of children starving in the night, of people freezing to death on the plains has faded. People are coming back and they say, "We've got to have a new thing," a program that would do away with the safety nets of the 1930s. It is actually an intellectual movement.

So, what's the idea? The idea is that all that came out of the 1930s was an entitlement program to which lazy and non-producing people could just simply sign up and they'd be taken care of for life by the government. The actual history of why it was the way it was, and where it came from, and who it served, and why it was adopted, and what it was in opposition to, all of that is forgotten. And all we're supposed to look at now are the entitlements, entitlements that we would like to, or that they would like to, eradicate.

The New Deal

Of course, they are going to eradicate all the social programs, not just the ones that came with the New Deal. So, the plan would be, all the programs that hit Indian Country, that support everything in Indian Country, are on the block. They're on the table, and somebody's got a meat cleaver, and they like to chop.

But there's a problem. There's always been a problem. In a democracy, destroying the social network is expensive. Once you start cutting these programs, people start hurting. People who start hurting stand up and start complaining. The next thing you know, they start voting.

This is the revolt that we are seeing in Latin America. The World Bank and International Monetary Fund have been visiting programs upon those countries, demanding that they not have any social programs, that they not use their money to support education, that they not subsidize food, that they not subsidize medicine, that they only pay their debts to the banks, and that they abandon—it's called "structural adjustment"—that they abandon the people in the interest of foreign debts.

And what's happened? In country after country, they're voting in people who are telling the United States, "Go home, Yankee. We don't need you anymore."

Now the same thinkers want to bring that to the United States and, of course, over here people have a much longer history of not remembering what it was like to starve and freeze in the dark than they have in Latin American.

Creating Wealth

In the dominant population, I imagine that the momentum for that great idea will go on for a little while, but I would like to make a suggestion about Indian Country. When you are in any type of retirement seminars in the wealthy cities for people who have good incomes, the wealthy seminar people always turn their topic to the issue of how to produce wealth, how to create wealth. That's a drumbeat in the upper middle-class issue on retirement, to create wealth.

When was the last time you saw anybody have a seminar about how to create wealth in Indian Country? It's not the same thing as generating income. You can generate money, but does the money create anything that creates money itself? Does it create anything that creates social benefits itself? Does it have inherent value? Is it wealth which you create with your money?

And I have to say that I think that in Indian Country, we have infrastructure. There are buildings. There are roads. We've done a wonderful job in lots of places. Indian Country really pays attention to old people, to children, to education, to a whole range and list of things. And, with the monies that have come in, there has been some attention paid to jobs, but we do need to shift this to two other areas.

We need to create wealth, and we need to create an issue around subsistence—that cushion, that something above rock bottom, that the community has, that the community produces for itself, that gives it identity, that makes the caring and sharing—the cultural heritage a reality. In addition to that, that way of thinking needs to be integrated into a twenty-first century way of being in the world.

Outsourcing

I'm not abandoning the idea that we have to have careful outside investments. But in addition to that I think we need to think about internal investments.

So far, although there are a lot of people looking at a lot of ways of doing that—and I'm not scolding people about this because Indian Country is better than lots of places—there still needs to be, first off, a conversation about what kind of economic growth is appropriate for the kinds of places that we live.

Now, Indian Country is so diverse. You have little colonies inside of cities. You have places very remote on Indian reservations that nobody can even get to. And then you have all kinds of things in between there. You have reservations thirty miles from town, sixty miles, eighty miles, whatever. But many places need to reorient their thinking to ask fundamental questions. Given the circumstances that we're in, what's the kind of development that we need for our circumstances?

It has to be realistic.

You have to look and say, what kinds of economic development is available for rural people now? And it has to be realistic in the sense that it's not the way it used to be anymore.

I've been very struck with the fact that Indian Country is now in the mainstream of American economic life. Every morning, my reservation emanates great numbers of UPS trucks carrying stuff in and carrying stuff out. We need to ask ourselves what things should they be carrying in, and what things should they be carrying out.

And this has to be, I would hope at some point or another, because I think it's really important. We have to ask ourselves what sorts of things that benefit society are they bringing in and are they taking out. I really don't think, on the whole, that we can begin to end this entertainment locus, this entertainment thing. In the end, we need to have an economy like all other economies. It needs to serve our people. Indian national economies need to serve our people. It needs to be a real economy. We need to produce things other people need, and we need to produce highly skilled things so that our people can prosper from that.

Never Forget

The main elements about our colonization—and let us not ever forget our colonization—was that we were to be rendered as children, unable to take care of ourselves. Self-sufficiency doesn't only mean that you raise your own food, and heat, and housing. Self-sufficiency means that you have the capacity, the intellectual cultural capacity, to meet all your needs, to meet your economic needs, to meet your political needs, to meet your social needs.

It's a more complex and broader kind of mandate. I think in many places we have moved very far forward in our thinking and in having people that can do stuff in that area. But we've got lots of work to do yet.

Our communities have been subjected to policies that were intended to infantilize them, and especially to infantilize them economically. We need to reverse that. This is actually kind of a modest proposal. I'm not proposing a revolutionary thing at all.

I'm proposing that we think through how we can help the people, in all those various conditions that we find them in, so that they can do the appropriate things that enable them to become self-sufficient. And by self-sufficient, I mean the broadest term of self-sufficiency. I don't mean that they chop wood and raise gardens—except, it's okay with me for those people who can chop wood and raise gardens. Nothing wrong with that. But, in addition to that, we need people who have community activities that can generate dollars, and people who can reproduce themselves in a social way.

Two Messages

I'm saying that because I had two messages, if you'll remember.

My first message is that I think that we're going to see economic hard times. My second message is that, sometimes, economic hard times have been opportunity moments for people and in Native communities. So if the hard times come, I don't want to see our people lie down in defeat just because of that. This could be an opportunity for people, and I kind of expect it will be.

If five years from now we gather together, or you see me somewhere and you say, "Hey, what happened to that depression?" I will be completely at your mercy. But if we are having it, you'll know that you would have been better off taking that kind of advice home. You'd be better off anyway even if we never had a depression. But it would have been better off to take that kind of advice home.

In my profession, our job is to talk to people who try to understand how the world is working. I have lots of contacts with people who are recognized as knowledgeable so I can make this statement to you. Some of the world's best economists think we're approaching a crisis. It is very widely thought that we are. But they're not thinking about Indian Country. We have very few economists that actually worry about Indian Country. If they were worried about Indian Country though, I think they would give us the same kind of advice.

We need to produce the kind of wealth that sustains people in hard times, and it's not too early to ask people to start thinking about it.

Fortunately, there are a few places around where people are working on it so we need to pay attention to what they're doing, and maybe gain a certain amount of inspiration from them.

▼ ▼ ▼

John C. Mohawk, Ph.D., *was an author and professor in the Center for the Americas at the State University at Buffalo, New York. He was the Director of Indigenous Studies at the Center. He was also founder and director of the Iroquois White Corn Project and the Pinewoods Café, which are located on the Cattaraugus Territory of the Seneca Nation in Western New York. Find more of his recent writings at the project's web site www.prophecyandsurvival.com.*

Mohawk was editor for Akwesasne Notes *from 1967 to 1983 and editor of* Daybreak, *a national magazine which focused on indigenous topics, from 1987 to 1995. He also served as a delegate for the Six Nations Iroquois Confederacy to the conflict on the Ganienkeh Indian Territory in 1975, a delegate on a fact finding trip to Teheran during the American Embassy hostage crisis in 1980, a negotiator for the Mohawk Nation during the crisis at Racquette Point in 1981, a member of the committee that helped negotiate the* Salamanca Settlement Act of 1988, *and a designated representative from the Haudenosaunee to the Oka Crisis in Southern Quebec in 1990. He was a founding board member of the Seventh Generation Fund and the Indian Law Resource Center.*

About the Editors

Kara Briggs, Yakama, is an award-winning journalist and writer who worked for nearly twenty years in daily newspapers before joining the American Indian Policy and Media Initiative as its associate director and editor. She was an invited participant in the founding round table an currently serves as associate director for the project.

She is the primary editor and contributor of *Shoot the Indian: Media, Misperception and Native Truth*. She also contributed two original chapters.

Her experience includes writing a national health column for *Indian Country Today* and investigating public and private agencies for The Oregonian, one of the West's most aggressive newspapers, while developing feature stories that took readers inside Native and other communities. She extensively investigated Bureau of Indian Affairs schools for Indian children.

She is a former president of the Native American Journalists Association and Unity: Journalists of Color, which is a coalition of four minority journalists organization and represents 10,000 journalists. She also is a public speaker, frequently invited to keynote Native American conferences on health and the environment, and to speak at journalism conferences and universities about media ethics and race.

She was a 2004 fellow in the Minority Writer's Seminar of the National Conference of Editorial Writers Foundation, and a 2004 participant in the Freedom Forum's Justice and Journalism seminar on law, Indians and the media. In 2003, she was a Fellow of the Salzburg Institute in Austria, studying international human rights laws.

Her knowledge of urban development was recognized when she was extensively quoted in Harvard professor Robert D. Putnam's book *Better Together: Restoring the American Community* (2004). She graduated with a bachelor's degree in English from Whitworth College.

Ronald D. Smith is chairman of the Communication Department at Buffalo State College, coordinating the work of fifteen full-time and about twenty part-time faculty members in journalism, broadcasting, public relations, advertising and communication studies. He serves as director of the American Indian Policy & Media Initiative.

As a professor of public communication, he teaches undergraduate and graduate courses in public relations strategy, writing, case studies, research and related areas. He has worked as a public relations manager, newspaper reporter and editor, and Navy journalist during the Vietnam War. He also has served as a public relations consultant in public relations planning and crisis communication, and he has provided media training for many nonprofit organizations.

He has written three widely-used textbooks: *Strategic Planning for Public Relations* (2nd edition, 2005 Erlbaum); *Becoming a Public Relations Writer* (3rd edition, in press; Erlbaum); and (as co-author) *MediaWriting* (3rd edition, in press Erlbaum). He also has written *Introduction to Language and Communication: A Primer on Human and Media Communication for the University of the United Arab Emirates* (2004, Buffalo State). He is an editor and contributor for *Shoot the Indian: Media, Misperception and Native Truth.*

He is an accredited member of the Public Relations Society of America and has served as chapter president and district chair. He has been honored as chapter "Practitioner of the Year" and was nominated for the 2006 "Outstanding Educator" national award. He holds a bachelor's degree in English education (Lock Haven State College) and a master's degree in public relations (Syracuse University).

José Barreiro, Taino, is an author, scholar and intellectual activist with thirty years dedicated to the service of Native people. He serves currently as Assistant Director for Research at the Smithsonian National Museum of the American Indian.

His early work in Native issues spans from the co-editing of *Akwesasne Notes*, the primary Native publication of its time (1974-1984) to his two decades of Akwe:kon Press at Cornell University (1984-2003), where his active leadership and supervision generated a creative workshop of conferences, books, internships, museum exhibits, journals and community extension projects with hemispheric proportion. In the last several years he helped redesign *Indian Country Today* into a leading Native American news source, and he served as its senior editor and chief editorial writer.

At Cornell University for the nineteen previous years, he helped forge the American Indian Program at Cornell University, where he served as associate director and editor-in-chief of Akwe:kon Press and its journal Native Americas.

His book, *View from the Shore: American Indian Perspectives on the Quincentenary,* was a seminal work in the discourse of the 1992/500-year Anniversary of the Columbus Voyage. Barreiro also was an early observer and promoter of the entrance by Native peoples into the United Nations' processes of international recognition and assistance, which he documents in is book *Basic Call to Consciousness.* In 1974, he covered the intense government prosecution of American Indian Movement leaders after the incident at Wounded Knee, S.D. for *Akwesasne Notes.*

American Indian Policy
and Media Initiative

The American Indian Policy and Media Initiative is based in the Communication Department of Buffalo State College in New York and at the Tulalip Tribes' reservation in Washington. It's focus is on the intersection of policy and media, which it analyzes and critiques while working to strengthen media coverage of issues related to Native America. The Initiative also seeks to gather leading thinkers in Indian Country and the news media to consider the impact of news coverage of Native America on government policy concerning American Indians.

The Initiative grows out of a collaboration between the Communication Department and Native journalists and educators. Tim Johnson, Mohawk, and José Barreiro, Taino, founded the Initiative with Ronald D. Smith, as director. The Initiative now includes Kara Briggs, Yakama, who is associate director. It is funded by Buffalo State College, the Lannan Foundation and several Native nations.

The Initiative has sponsored research and reporting on public opinion concerning American Indians and Native-related policy issues, as well as content analysis of media reports on Indian topics.

Its public phase began in June 2005 with a Round Table meeting in Buffalo that included retired Senator Ben Nighthorse Campbell, then Chairman Anthony Pico of the Viejas Band of Kumeyaay Indians, Chief Jim Ransom of the Saint Regis Mohawks, writer Suzan Shown Harjo, and other tribal leaders, cultural commentators, and Native journalists.

Discussing issues ranging from the congressional bribery scandal involving Jack Abramoff to coverage of tribal gaming, the participants agreed that the Initiative could foster accuracy about media coverage of tribal nations and Native Americans by critiquing the media and also by placing commentary about Indian issues in the media.

In 2006, the initiative co-sponsored a conference in Washington, D.C. with the American Friends Committee. The Initiative is preparing to co-sponsor a successor conference.

The American Indian Policy and Media Initiative also has placed several newspaper commentaries on topics related to public policy and Native issues. Initiative leaders have assisted newspaper editorial pages in developing responsible, balanced viewpoints on Native subjects. The Initiative also has conducted a research study on civic engagement and tribal relations for the National Museum of the American Indian.

Keep up with the Initiative's ongoing work at,
www.AmericanIndanInitiative.buffalostate.edu.

▼ ▼ ▼

Index